JAMES THOMPSON

JOURNEY
BOOKS

An SPC Publication
Austin, Texas 78765

Look for these additional Journey book titles coming this year:

What Every Family Needs, or Whatever Happened to Mom, Dad, and the Kids
Carl Brecheen & Paul Faulkner

Chosen for Riches—A Life-Related Exposition of Ephesians
Bob Hendren

Life Beyond Darkness—The Love Letters of John
Robert Shank

A complete Teacher's Manual/Resource Kit for use with this paperback is available from your religious bookstore or the publisher.

Unless otherwise indicated, scripture quotations are from the *Revised Standard Version of the Bible,* copyrighted 1946, 1952, and 1971 by the Division of Christian Education, National Council of Churches, and used by permission.

Library of Congress Catalog Card Number 77-79338
ISBN 8344-0095-2

CONTENTS

Foreword

FOREWORD

Fellowship is second on God's spiritual "Hall Of Fame" items! Only doctrine comes before it. Did the Holy Spirit list spiritual matters in the order of their importance? Probably any answer given cannot be proven; but suffice it to say neither is the Holy Spirit a careless or thoughtless scribe. After all, how can one have "fellowship" unless it is based on the proper truth? After obedience to doctrine rightfully comes fellowship.

In the infancy of the church Luke declared, "And they continued steadfastly in the apostles' doctrine and fellowship, and in breaking of bread, and in prayers" (Acts 2:42, KJV). No body of people can do less today and still lay claim to being "of Christ."

"Apostles' doctrine" imparts great mental comfort. How can error be practiced if implicit obedience is given to "thus sayeth the Lord"? Who can do wrong being right?

But can one be "right" only that far and still be the ideal of God? Does not doctrine instruct as to "fellowship"? Jesus is most important; but the followers of Jesus are also important. Life is not all vertical—any more than it is only horizontal. The cross points toward heaven—from earth; it also points to man while on earth. In an impervious age that has its "I-don't-want-to-get-involved" attitude, it is vitally essential to reexamine basic teachings on fellowship.

James Thompson is an excellent writer, a sensitive student of the word, and one who challenges to the fullness of thoughts on this subject. As he brings one closer to Christ, he readily knows that he brings all of us closer to one another. In Jesus, he strives to make it easier for us to say to one another, "I love you." He wants the "Me Decade," as he refers to it, to become the "We Decade"—Christ, you, me.

May this study lead to that holy end. God bless, as you now embark on an exciting and earnest study of a beautiful subject—Fellowship with the Savior And the Saints. We earnestly hope that you have both.

Jim Bill McInteer

Jim Bill McInteer
West End Church of Christ
Nashville, Tennessee

A CALL TO FELLOWSHIP
chapter 1

"For I long to see you . . . that we may be mutually encouraged" Romans 1:11-12

What if an observer came to the church where you worship to make a careful analysis of the church's life in fellowship? He is a specialist in studying how groups work together, and he intends to compare your congregation's life as a community with other groups such as the civic club, the lodge, the garden club, and the college fraternity or sorority. What would you expect him to discover?

The observer examines how we relate to one another when we come together for worship. He notices how we interact with each other away from our church assemblies to see if we really share in a common life with other Christians. He quickly notices such things as our group loyalties, our wiliingness (or unwillingness) to support each other in time of need, and the amount of time we spend enjoying the company of others in the local church. He also pays special attention to how well those who sit by each other during the assembly Sunday after Sunday really know each other.

Such a study might reveal some frightening insights into *our life together* in the local church.

What would we discover about ourselves? Several years ago some churches allowed themselves to be analyzed in just this way. What they learned was very disturbing. In a series of interviews the members were asked such things as, "How many of those present in the worship service do you know personally?" The great majority of church members had to admit that they knew a very small percentage of the people. Those who gathered for worship on Sunday were an anonymous group of worshipers. They were not a genuine community of people prepared to bear the burdens of one another.

"Many go to church as they would go to the movie theater."

Equally disturbing was the fact that many of those who were questioned expressed little interest in becoming more involved in the lives of other members. They thought that such social relationships had very little to do with the Christian life. They were satisfied with their own circle of church friends and felt no need to reach out and establish a wider circle of relationships.

When asked why they came to worship, the members responded that they came only for the sake of their own spiritual life and personal salvation. They did not come to establish a better fellowship with other Christians. As one person said, "Many go to church as they would go to the movie theater." It is as if they were satisfied with their personal spiritual life without being a part of a fellowship.

INDISPENSABLE FELLOWSHIP

If the local church becomes a near-anonymous group of worshipers, we miss an indispensable part of what the Christian faith can do to enrich our lives. Paul affirms the indispensable value of warmth and fellowship in his letter to Roman Christians: "For I long to see you . . . that we may be mutually encouraged by each other's faith, both yours and mine" (1:11-12).

Anyone who has been fortunate enough to be nurtured in a church where there was genuine warmth knows that we cannot lightly dispense with a strong sense of community.

Many of us can think back to occasions when the local church came to our side when there was illness in the family. I can recall moving to a new town where we were very lonely until friends in the church "took us in." It was the one place where we found lasting friendships based on common values and a way of life. Undoubtedly many of us have found some close ties in the church that we could not replace.

Nevertheless, we share in a dilemma. We may recognize that fellowship is a very good thing, but it is very difficult to maintain a strong fellowship in many congregations. We are far more mobile and far busier than we were in former generations. Many of us live great distances from the place of worship,

9

preventing us from having easy access to the church community.

ANONYMOUS WORSHIPERS

New families move into our congregation, and others move away. In this situation it is tempting for us to avoid getting involved in a close relationship to the church. And if we worship in a large congregation, we find it very easy to become divided into smaller groups which have no relationship to members outside our small circle. We may not be intentionally divisive or exclusive as we move within the smaller group. Yet it is easy to be cut off from the rest of the church. And when this isolation occurs, we do become an anonymous group of worshipers.

These problems make it difficult for us to live as a caring community. If we are an anonymous group of worshipers on Sunday, it is possible that we do not compare favorably as a community with the civic club or fraternity! The church becomes the place where we come *only* to meet God and nourish our spirits, and *not* the place where we meet each other, the people of God.

PREOCCUPIED WITH SELF

I am convinced that it is not only the fast pace of life that prevents us from being a more genuine fellowship. The church is also prevented from being a caring fellowship by a failure to appreciate the biblical teaching about our life together. We will never be a genuine community as long as we are a people who care only for our own spiritual welfare.

Our social critic has described the 1970s as the "Me Decade." People who have given up on organized religion have turned to radical humanism to "get in touch with themselves." Such programs as Transcendental Meditation and Yoga claim to offer personal awareness. This tendency easily leads a person to think only of himself—his private experiences and his own personal development.

While we cannot object to the idea of personal growth, we can object to a preoccupation with *self* that leads us to withdraw from the needs of others. This same temptation has led others to turn to drugs in order to withdraw from a wider network of relationships. The danger is that we can become so involved with ourselves that we cease to care for others. As one writer said, today's emphasis on self awareness has "made caring seem like losing."

We can become so involved with ourselves that we cease to care for others.

This emphasis on self has its religious overtones. Sometimes sincere people become so preoccupied with a "personal relationship with Jesus Christ" that the church community seems to be insignificant. In other instances Christians become so concerned with the experience or "feeling" of the Spirit that they withdraw from the larger community and retreat into private experience or into small groups. Impatience with the organized church even leads some to become fragmented into smaller groups where they try to exercise a freedom from responsibility to the larger community.

Anyone who is convinced that Christianity involves only personal growth and the vertical rela-

11

tionship to Jesus Christ can easily decide that fellow-ship is irrelevant to his Christian life.

The "Me Decade" constantly threatens Christianity. We need to return to the Scriptures in order to learn that God has called us to a life in community. The God who broke down human barriers once and for all through Jesus Christ calls us to be "members of one another." And the Bible, as we shall see later, provides the definition of real fellowship.

INDIVIDUALISTS AT CORINTH

In Paul's day there were Christians at Corinth who seemed to be interested only in their private relationship to God experienced in spiritual gifts (1 Cor. 12; 14), in baptism (1 Cor. 12:13), and in the Lord's Supper (1 Cor. 10:16). But Paul reminded them that they were a part of a body. These individualists at Corinth, as we shall see in a later chapter, had torn the community apart (1 Cor. 1:10-15).

If we today are interested only in our private relationship with God, we cannot bring together a loving fellowship. What we need, therefore, is to recover the biblical viewpoint about our life together in order to see what kind of fellowship God calls us to be.

Perhaps we do not always see the urgency of becoming a more genuine fellowship. We often think of fellowship as a social occasion and not the real work of the church. We sometimes describe fellowship as if it only involved having our best friends over for dinner. Or we think of it as the occasional class party. We may have even described the casual conversation before and after worship as a time of fellowship.

If fellowship is nothing more than these occasions,

it lacks depth and substance. The Bible describes dimensions of fellowship that extend far beyond these occasions. These added dimensions allow us to see the urgency of our life together.

GOD'S SPECIAL COMMUNITY

Visualize Israel's children encamped at the foot of Sinai. They were a sojourning community, bound for their land of promise. In the New Testament the Greek word *koinonia* describes the steadfast fellowship between God and his wilderness children throughout every century. It also characterizes the close relationship that is to be nurtured and sustained among the people of God. The emphasis of the word focuses on sharing a common relationship. We participate together in God's family, his present-day community.

The language of the common (*koine*) people in the Hellenistic world was koine (*koi-'na*) Greek. It denoted something shared in common with others: common language, common ownership, common relationships, common ideas, or that which concerned all.

Of the many forms of the word *common*, the concept of *community* is easily the most dynamic. From the days of the patriarchs to the twentieth-century church, God has always possessed a special community of people whom he calls his own. This word will be explored in depth in later chapters.

THE BIBLE AND FELLOWSHIP

The Bible says much to remind us that our Christianity was never meant to be lived alone. We are reminded by John that a relationship with God leads

13

to "fellowship with one another" (1 John 1:3). We read of those who reached out to one another with "the right hand of fellowship" (Gal. 2:9). Paul rejoices at one point over the "fellowship in the gospel" (Phil. 1:5, KJV) which a congregation provided. One of the earliest statements about the life of the infant church was that the disciples "devoted themselves to the apostles' teaching and fellowship, to the breaking of bread and the prayers" (Acts 2:42).

These records remind us just how seriously the early church took its fellowship. It was never an optional part of the Christian life. The earliest Christians could never have imagined a Christianity that consisted only in a "personal relationship" with Jesus Christ. Any personal relationship with God apart from a vital relationship to the church would have been empty.

Our Christianity was never meant to be lived alone.

We catch glimpses of the vitality of the church's fellowship throughout the New Testament. We notice Paul's emphasis on corporate life when he reminds the Corinthians, "For by one spirit we were all baptized into one body—Jews or Greeks, slaves or free—and all were made to drink of one Spirit" (1 Cor. 12:13). And in the same chapter he says of the body of Christ, "If one member suffers, all suffer together; if one member is honored, all rejoice together" (12:26). Similarly, James describes the church as the people who confess their faults to each other and "pray for one another" (James 5:16).

We notice, therefore, a community which is

14

known for its hospitality and enjoys reaching out to others. The church was the one place where people could find genuine warmth.

How does this teaching about fellowship relate to the church when assembled for worship? How does our prayer life relate to the life of the whole community? Do our hymns, our practice of assembling at regular times, and our life away from the assembly enable us to share life together? The Bible summons us to examine our fellowship in the light of its teaching.

This issue of the relationship of the individual and the group is a very old issue indeed. Apparently that issue was faced repeatedly in the early church, for it was often Paul's task to remind new and struggling churches that the biblical faith is lived in community. Wherever individualism tended to break down the community, Paul seems to have reminded his readers that God had called them into a "fellowship" (1 Cor. 10:16). Where the "strong" within the community wanted to ignore the "weak," Paul reminded them that God had called them into a Christian community (Rom. 14:1–15:13).

In Paul's day, as in ours, there were individualists who were content to live anonymously apart from the fellowship. Since the issues of Paul's day are very much like our own, we can learn much from examining them.

A PLACE TO BELONG

We have noticed how seriously the early church understood her task of being a real Christian community. There was, in fact, none like it. There were many religious rivals to the Christians. Many claimed to provide what was offered by Christianity. The rivals claimed to offer hope for future salvation and a new start in life. But what they did *not* offer was a life together. The church alone met this vital need.

One great classical scholar has suggested that this sense of being a community explains why Christianity had such a remarkable growth in the first century. In ancient times there were millions of uprooted people who came to the cities trying to improve their lot in life. They were separated from their families and other loved ones. And it was only in the church that they found a home.

Within the Christian community there was a sense of warmth: someone was interested in them both here and hereafter. Here the stranger found a place where the people were "members of one another!" It is no wonder that the church enjoyed such growth. There was no other community quite like it. The fellowship of the church meant far more than inviting one's close friends to a social gathering; it meant providing a little warmth to people who wanted to belong.

The church in ancient times found the secret of its strength in providing the kind of community that was available nowhere else. Does not this fact suggest that we today should have something to offer in our own time?

We have seen increasing evidence in recent years that people need to belong and are looking for *a place to be valued*. As a result of the mobility in our society this need to belong has become increasingly a factor to large segments of our population. Our large cities are composed of masses of people who are marked by anonymity. The group ties which may have existed in the smaller towns have been broken. The ties to the extended family hardly exist.

A CALL TO FELLOWSHIP

This uprootedness has left people today, as in ancient times, without any sense of community. Perhaps, if the ancient church could minister to this need for belonging, today's church can minister to the same desire and at the same time regain its vitality.

Sociologists have shown that mobility and rootlessness can have destructive consequences on our lives. We must have something to bring security into our lives. Where people are uprooted, family life disintegrates and the crime rate increases. If we are constantly subject to rapid change, we need an area of security somewhere in our lives where we can feel at home.

It is at this point that the church has an important role. *The church can minister to loneliness and uprootedness by providing a community and a sense of belonging.*

The church provided this to uprooted people in the first century. We learn from the message of scripture that God calls us to be the same kind of fellowship today. We are to be that unique community found nowhere else!

A MUSTARD SEED PEOPLE

chapter 2

"Let both grow together until the harvest."

Matthew 13:30

There is a widespread belief in many circles that, while Jesus taught many useful things, there is little connection between Jesus and the community of believers we call the church. It is as if he had given stirring lessons on the love of God for the individual, but cared little for the establishment of the church.

When Jesus is seen in this way, such moral teachings as the Sermon on the Mount are interpreted as a lifestyle for individual believers, not guidelines for life in the church. His message about the kingdom is thought to relate to use as isolated individuals, not as a community of believers.

This view that Jesus can be divorced from the church has been persistent. Indeed, it has been so persistent that we must ask in this chapter: What was

Jesus' message concerning the church community?

If we are to understand the place of the church in Jesus' teaching, we must first recall the obvious fact that Jesus was a Jew.

A Jewish boy in Nazareth who received the normal education afforded in the synagogue heard early in life about God's special plans for Israel. Undoubtedly Jesus heard in the synagogue about the call of Abraham and about God's special covenant with Israel at Mount Sinai. His teachers must have emphasized that God's covenant was not merely with select individuals, but with the whole people of God. No doubt Jesus went to the synagogue regularly to participate in corporate worship, where he shared in the recitation of the words, "Hear, O Israel, our Lord is one."

Jesus experienced from childhood the corporate life of faith. And his teachings appear to have been richly flavored by his training and early life in the community.

GATHERED TOGETHER

Jesus' intention to establish a church is made explicit in only one passage in the New Testament. In Matthew 16:18, after Peter has confessed that Jesus is the promised Christ, Jesus replies, "You are Peter, and on this rock I will build my church."

The original word for "church" is *ekklesia,* a term which would have been meaningful to Jesus' hearers. The term would have suggested his intention to build a new community of faith.

Jewish listeners would have recalled that in the Old Testament there were many references to God's congregation. They would have recalled that it was with a gathered congregation that God had made his covenant at Sinai. They would have known that their spiritual life centered around that gathering known as a "synagogue" where they met in public worship.

Thus, when Jesus announced his intention to build the church, his hearers knew that he had not come to dismiss the life God's people shared together. They knew that just as God had entered into a covenant with his congregation in the Old Testament, Jesus intended to establish a new community.

THE KING AND HIS PEOPLE

Since the church is mentioned only once in the Gospels, one must look elsewhere to see the role which the church played in the entire teaching of Jesus.

The central aspect of the teaching of Jesus was his proclamation of the coming of the kingdom. The gospel of Mark seems to summarize the entire message of Jesus when it records that Jesus came into Galilee at the beginning of his ministry saying, "The time is fulfilled, and the kingdom of God is at hand" (Mark 1:15). Every Jew believed that God was in fact king. "The Lord will reign for ever and ever" (Exod. 15:18).

The Jewish people at the time of Jesus lived under the yoke of the occupying armies of Rome. They believed that in the future God would be king in a more dynamic way. Although he was already king, he was to set up his kingdom in a way that would leave no doubt about him.

Those who heard Jesus' announcement that "the kingdom of God is at hand" must have recalled the hope expressed in Daniel 2:44: "God will set up a

20

kingdom which shall never be destroyed." When Jesus made his dramatic announcement, many listeners hoped that their dreams as a people had been fulfilled; the kingdom was "at hand."

What kind of kingdom had Jesus announced? How would that kingdom become a reality in the lives of the people?

The word "kingdom" suggests to most of us the idea of a specific territory or a political state. But to Jesus' Jewish listeners the word suggested something different. The Hebrew word for kingdom meant literally "the reign of God" or "the rule of God." When the people thought of God's kingdom, they thought of God's rule in the lives of men.

Thus, the kingdom is not something which men may build; it is God's ruling activity which "comes upon us" (Luke 11:20) and establishes its rule in human lives.

When we consider how central the kingdom was for Jesus, we realize the importance of the community of faith in Jesus' teaching. The kingdom never happens in a vacuum; if there is to be a kingdom, there must be subjects in that kingdom. Just as God's rule in the Old Testament required a chosen community of people, Jesus' teaching about the kingdom in the New Testament implies the existence of the community of faith.

A MUSTARD SEED PEOPLE

What kind of community did Jesus envision? What are the laws of its growth? What kind of people will comprise the kingdom?

The parables provide us with answers to these questions. Jesus' parables were taken from life, and they addressed questions spoken and thought by his listeners. They give us an insight into the problems which confronted Jesus and his disciples in the years of his public ministry.

The disciples must have looked unimpressive. So one of the most serious problems which Jesus' disciples faced was *doubt*. Could this little band of disciples really be that glorious kingdom announced long ago in the book of Daniel? There were no community leaders among them and no one from the aristocracy. Perhaps no one had heard of them beyond the borders of insignificant Galilee. Already Jesus' announcement concerning the kingdom had met with indifference and even rejection (Mark 6:6; John 6:66). Could this wretched band of disciples really be the kingdom? Was there any future to such a community?

The Hebrew word for kingdom meant literally "the rule of God."

To these doubts Jesus had an answer. He compared the kingdom of God to a grain of mustard seed which was proverbial for its smallness. His hearers knew of the incredible transformation of the microscopic mustard seed into a huge bush—large enough to become a nesting place for the birds (Mark 4:30-32). There was no better analogy for the coming of the kingdom.

Jesus' band of disciples was no success story in the earliest days of his mission. This community was certainly no model of power and glory. Was his community ever to amount to anything? "Yes!" said Jesus, "With the same certainty that the tiny mustard seed becomes a great tree."

What kind of community of disciples did Jesus picture? The parable of the mustard seed reminds us that it was to be a growing community.

A KINGDOM DESTINED TO GROW

The kingdom was to be a community that would never accept failure. This assurance in the future of the community is an important part of other parables of Jesus.

The parable of the sower (Mark 4:3-8) reflects the frustrations of the one who had sown the word. He had sown the message on the beaten path, on the rock ground, and in the midst of thorns. The message of the kingdom of God had been crowded out.

Jesus agreed with his frustrated disciples that not every attempt to sow the word would meet with huge success. But Jesus' parable did not stop with the admission of frustration. He told also of that fourth soil which brought forth "thirtyfold and sixtyfold and a hundredfold" (Mark 4:8).

In the same way, we may fail in three attempts out of four. But there is always that fourth attempt which bears the unbelievable bumper crop—thirtyfold and sixtyfold and a hundredfold. And it is that bumper crop which makes our work entirely worthwhile.

What kind of kingdom did Jesus anticipate? Was it to be marked by failure? Did it give up when success was not apparent? The parable of the sower was Jesus' expression of absolute confidence that his community, this motley band, was really the kingdom of God. Jesus' community was destined to grow.

But how shall it grow? Does the growth of this community depend on the organizational skills of its leaders or on the talents of its members?

"The kingdom of God," says Jesus, "is as if a man should scatter seed upon the ground, and should sleep and rise night and day, and the seed should sprout and grow, he knows not how" (Mark 4:26). No, the growth of the kingdom does not depend merely on the talents of the members; men don't build the kingdom. The farmer plants and cultivates his seed in the full assurance that the harvest depends on God. It is upon God that the growth of the kingdom depends. It is he who gives the increase.

The kingdom, then, is not abandoned by God and left to its own devices. God's power expressed through his people is the source of the kingdom's growth.

SHALL WE WEED THE KINGDOM?

One fact about Jesus' community must have appeared particularly disturbing to many dedicated disciples. People from every conceivable background were entering into this community. Jesus seemed to exercise little discretion in making the call to discipleship. Even within the inner circle of disciples there was one disciple who had been a tax collector, a collaborator with the Roman government. There was also a Zealot, one of those revolutionary types.

The Master's followers were unlike any religious community these people had ever seen. The Pharisees and the Sadducees had standards! Even the pagan religious associations were limited to people of a certain economic standing. But anyone could belong to this community! And, no doubt, there were some people within the community whose reputations could have given Jesus and his disciples a bad name. This fact led to the obvious question: "Shouldn't we begin to weed out the community? Shouldn't we be more selective in regard to whom the invitation is extended?"

It was to that kind of question that Jesus responded with the parable of the weeds (Matt. 13:24-30). Jesus told about a farmer's frustration of finding out, after he had already done his sowing, that an enemy had planted weeds among his wheat.

Jesus' listeners with their background in agriculture could appreciate the dilemma. They knew if the farmer had gone to weed out his crops during the growing season, he would have destroyed the entire crop. The weeds, at this stage in growth, could not be distinguished from the good wheat. Only one choice was open to the farmer: Let the wheat and the weeds grow together until the harvest. Only at the harvest could the good and the bad be separated.

The wheat and weeds were an apt analogy for the kingdom of God. To those who wanted to be more selective in receiving people into the kingdom, Jesus was saying, "Let both grow together until the harvest" (Matt. 13:30). It was his counsel against a premature weeding of the community when the authentic and hypocritical are all but indistinguishable.

The community of Jesus is never going to be characterized by its *sameness*. His disciples must take care in their weeding, lest they tear the community apart. It was Jesus' way of saying that his community will always be a mixed community; the church will always have its sinners and hypocrites. Only at the harvest will the final separation take place.

Jesus made an identical point in the twin parable of the seine net (Matt. 13:47-50). To those who wanted to be selective in their proclamation, Jesus declared that they should be no more selective than a seine net which "gathered fish of every kind" (13:47). That is not to say, however, that bad fish are to be eaten. It does suggest the church is a mixture of the good and the bad; and it is God who will be responsible for making the final separation.

A FELLOWSHIP OF SINNERS

When the Jewish people wanted to think about the glories of the next life, they could imagine no more apt way of portraying heaven than the image of a great banquet. In the next life many would "come from east and west and sit at the table with Abraham, Isaac, and Jacob in the kingdom of heaven" (Matt. 8:11). In traditional Jewish expectation, heaven was compared to a great fellowship dinner.

In the teaching of Jesus this fellowship dinner was in progress. He announced that the kingdom of God was breaking in (Luke 11:20). In his ministry the wedding banquet was already taking place. Consequently, he refused to fast because he was like a bridegroom at his own wedding party (Mark 2:19-20). The good news of the kingdom was announced by Jesus, and he was inviting people to the fellowship meal (Matt. 22:1-14; Luke 14:16-24).

The Jews knew, as we do today, that mealtime is not only the time for nourishing our bodies; it is also a time for nourishing relationships. Families find mealtime an important occasion for being together. Social relationships are frequently solidified around the table, for the act of eating with someone is an act of acceptance and fellowship. This fact became quite evident in the early church, where the new unity found in Jesus Christ was often expressed by sharing in a common meal (Gal. 2:11-21).

It is for this reason that the Jews were horrified at Jesus' regular practice of eating with sinners. "This man receives sinners and eats with them," the Jews charged (Luke 15:2).

For the Jews of Jesus' day, the sinner was to be avoided. It was only with the pious that the religious Jew would share in a fellowship meal. Thus their most persistent criticism of Jesus was that he ate with sinners (Mark 2:16). Undoubtedly it was this practice which brought forth the accusation that Jesus was a *glutton* and a *drunkard* (Matt. 11-19), a "friend of tax collectors and sinners."

The parable of the mustard seed reminds us that it was to be a growing community.

One Bible scholar has suggested that it was Jesus' table fellowship with sinners which most enraged Jesus' countrymen and led to their decision to execute him. All sinners were to be avoided. The Jews looked forward, for example, to the ultimate destruction of the publicans—those collaborators with Rome—and other sinners. Then Jesus came and invited them into the fellowship of the kingdom. No one had been so daring in extending the invitation as to invite outcasts and sinners to share in the fellowship meal.

Why did Jesus risk the wrath of the religious people of his day by inviting sinners to share in the fellowship meal? It was the conviction that "those who are well have no need of a physician, but those who are sick" (Mark 2:17). When Jesus ate with these people, he was giving a demonstration lesson on the nature of God's kingdom. God's kingdom was not to become the exclusive club for the perfect. It was forever to extend the invitation of fellowship to the outcasts and to sinners.

Can the church be loyal to its Lord and ignore the dramatic implications of Jesus' message concerning the nature of the kingdom? The kingdom which Jesus initiated is a fellowship of citizens who are sinners saved by grace and committed to overcoming sin. Is his reign to be found today where religious people ignore those who need the physician most?

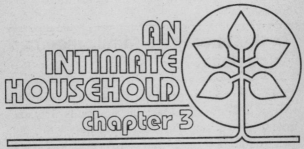

AN INTIMATE HOUSEHOLD
chapter 3

"He who does the will of God is my brother."
Mark 3:35

Jesus not only called men into a personal relationship with himself, he called them into a fellowship with each other.

There is a tendency today to employ terms from secular experience to describe the fellowship of Christians. Sometimes the athletic metaphor is used, and the church becomes a "team" intent on victory. Perhaps even more frequently, the church draws its terminology from the business world. The church is considered the corporation or business, and its leaders take on the function of corporate board members.

These terms may have a limited usefulness in reminding us that we are a part of a larger group. But they do not convey the depth and quality of the fellowship which Jesus intended. Athletic teams and corporations frequently function without the existence of close ties between members. The fellowship which Jesus intended cannot! It is of a different quality from the team spirit found on the athletic field or in the corporation.

The depth of fellowship which Jesus intended is nowhere more graphically illustrated than in Mark's narrative of Jesus' encounter with his mother and brothers.

In the church no family member is useless.

In the immediate context of this story, Jesus' activities in Galilee had become notorious. His enemies were accusing him of being in league with Satan. We are told that those who were especially close to Jesus (the Greek literally means "his people" and can apply to either his family or friends) came to take charge of him (Mark 3:20-21). It was being reported everywhere that "Jesus was out of his mind."

This common concern about Jesus provides the basis for our understanding of the poignant scene which follows in Mark 3:31-35. Jesus' family —his mother and his brothers—came to the place where he was teaching and called for him. But they received a strange reply. Rather than go out to meet them, Jesus replied to those who informed him of his family's visit, "Who are my mother and brothers?" It was his reminder that he had left home once for all and had embarked on his mission.

Then he looked around the room and answered, "Behold my mother and my brothers. He who does the will of God is my brother and sister and mother."

Though Jesus loved his mother, it was among his disciples that he found an expanded family.

AN INTIMATE HOUSEHOLD

Jesus' favorite image for the people of faith is that of the family. When we recall that Jesus described his disciples as a family, we see how inadequate the metaphors from business and athletics are for describing the people of God.

We have every reason to believe that Jesus experienced a good family life. Perhaps his consistent use of the term "Father" as a description of God suggests something of the quality of his family life. He knew that a family is far more cohesive and intimate than most organizations. He knew that families have in common the intimacies of shared suffering as well as shared joy. There could not have been a better metaphor for the community which surrounded Jesus. It knew the common life that only a family knows.

The church is in fact *God's household* (1 Tim. 3:15). This concept was especially potent among the early disciples. Discipleship had often come at the cost of giving up ties with their own families (Luke 14:25ff.; Matt. 8:21-22). For many, the church was their only family. They were more than teammates and more than fellow workers; they were a brotherhood (1 Pet. 2:17), and Christ was their older brother (Heb. 2:11ff.).

If the church loses this intimate sense of family life, it becomes an anonymous crowd of worshipers. It also loses an essential element of power which originally gave many people their security in an uncertain world.

In many spheres of life our existence has become increasingly depersonalized. Mobility has, in many instances, uprooted us from our family relationships. The computer has turned us into numbers in relation to our school and our employer. The church can serve its mission in this kind of world only if it understands itself as the family of God where individuals are bound by a relationship to the same Father.

GUIDELINES FOR FAMILY LIFE

In keeping with Jesus' imagery of the family, the term which Jesus uses for individual believers is "brother." At times the word can be used in a general sense to refer to the *needy* and the *helpless*, as in the story of the last judgment (Matt. 25:31-46). In other instances, however, Jesus uses the word "brother" for those who are born of the same spiritual womb. Consequently, in Matthew Jesus counsels his followers against bitter anger against a brother (5:22). He warns us against exercising judgment upon a brother (7:3) and demands that we be forgiving toward our brothers (18:15ff.).

Because the church is a family composed of brothers and sisters, there should be the unity that can overcome any kind of tension. However, even in the best of families there are times of tension. Discord is always the possibility where brothers and sisters live in close proximity to each other. Family unity does not just happen!

For this reason Jesus provides guidelines in Matthew 18 for the harmonious family of God. He does not present guidelines for a corporation, but guidelines for a family. The language concerns

Christians as children (Matt. 18:4-5), little ones (18:6, 10), and as brothers (18:15, 21). Jesus knew that it was not enough to speak of his people as a family; he knew that his people must learn the distinctive guidelines for family life.

Looking at these guidelines, we become aware of the supreme importance of each individual in the community. In 1 Corinthians 12:20-25 the individual is not measured merely by the function he performs. And he is not cast out when he is no longer able to fulfil his function.

Jesus indicates that every Christian is one of the little ones (Matt. 18:6, 10) for whom he cares. Sometimes the term "little ones" refers to children (18:6); at other times the expression refers to new members within the community (18:10). Nevertheless, the point is the same: those people whose function is limited are important.

Such people can never be reduced to numbers on a computer or even to numbers on a church roll. Their lives are so important that it is the business of the whole church to see that these seemingly insignificant people are never lost. People may become superfluous in other communities; but in the church no family member is useless.

WOE TO THE SEDUCERS

Consider, for instance, the warning in Matthew 18:6ff. about those who "cause (others) to sin." The Greek *skandalizo* ("cause to sin") meant "to set a trap." Here Jesus has in mind one in the community who causes another to lose his faith, and thus to be lost. To seduce another member into sin is so serious that Jesus pronounces his "woe" (18:7) upon any who become the source of temptation.

The church is to rid itself of those traps and seductions that might lead another into sin. We are our brothers' keepers in the Christian family! "Woe to the man by whom the temptation comes!" (18:7). The Christian fellowship is characterized by a caring attitude even toward those whose function seems insignificant.

Probably none of the disciples looked upon themselves as "seducers" leading their brothers into sin. And I doubt that we see ourselves in that light today. Yet seduction does occur.

Most such offenses occur in subtle and thoughtless ways. For example, the church can become so infatuated with increasing its attendance or membership that it fails to give attention to lonely people who need others to acknowledge them and demonstrate interest in them. It may even become so program-conscious that these little ones become a bother. Some of these little ones may at first be enthusiastic about the church's work, only to be *seduced* by the apathy of the other members.

Human communities may take a calloused attitude toward their dropouts. But the Christian fellowship is different. These little ones are important to the Father who calls us into fellowship.

EACH PERSON OF VALUE

How far does this caring attitude toward the little ones extend? The story of the lost sheep, as it appears in Matthew's gospel (18:10-14), is an answer to this question.

This story was taken directly from the agrarian life and customs of Jesus' hearers. His listeners knew

34

the shepherd regularly counted his sheep in the evening, and that even one lost sheep out of an average flock of a hundred would be disturbing. Thus, the story makes a fitting analogy for Jesus' teaching about the community.

What does the church do when it has lost one of its members? The parable provides an answer. The Christian is like the shepherd who went out to find the lost sheep. The church is never content with the ninety-nine who remain. Its responsibility extends to its lost sheep. Where the church is loyal to its Lord, it goes out to find those memberships who leave the fellowship.

Each of us stands between the forgiveness that is granted us and the forgiveness that is asked of us.

If the church were merely involved in a "numbers game," it might choose to replace its lost sheep by redoubling its efforts at evangelism. It might even find it easier to attract new members than to bring back its lost sheep.

Indeed, one of the problems with efforts at mass evangelism has been the "numbers game." Energies are sometimes expended on conversions at the expense of a loving concern toward those who leave the community.

The church's task in evangelistic efforts is *not* to be minimized; but the community founded by Christ is interested in more than numbers. It goes out to find lost sheep because "it is not the will of my Father who is in heaven that one of these little ones should perish" (Matt. 18:14).

FAMILY DISCIPLINE

Some people are lost to the church through the seductions of other members, as in those cases where a brother causes one of the little ones to stumble (Matt. 18:6, 10). But in other instances members are lost because of their own sin (18:15).

The instructions in Matthew 18:15ff. resume once more the language of family life. Here, the church is instructed about its behavior when one brother sins against another family member. The church, like any family, cannot live without its own *disciplined* family life.

How do you respond when your brother sins against you? The natural inclination is to return the offense. Injured pride, the malicious lie, destruction of one's reputation—all of these call for revenge. And in most human institutions the offense is returned.

Jesus' kingdom, however, lives by a different rule. It lives by love, not revenge. "Go and tell him his fault, between you and him alone," says Jesus (Matt. 18:15). But does one go in arrogance in order to destroy his brother? Jesus says, "If he listens to you, you have gained your brother" (18:15). The same loving spirit that sends a disciple out to find a lost sheep also moves him to go to the brother who has sinned against him.

The object of our attempt to go to our brother is not to satisfy our pride; it is to save him. His sin against us has made him no less important to us. Our first response is *not* to think of ourselves, but to think of his destiny.

The object of going to our brother to inform him of his sin is the same as when we avoid enticing him into sin or when we go out to find him when he is lost. It is to win him back to the Lord who called us.

The community which is callous toward its little ones—those who appear insignificant or troublesome—is futile. It may be like most human communities, but it is not the community which Christ called into being.

Even where this brother is a troublemaker, the guidelines laid down by Jesus are intended to rescue him. Jesus also describes other efforts at discipline. We may take witnesses with us in our efforts to reach him, and we may finally take the case before the whole church (18:16f.). We do not give up easily, because he is important. The community lives by its concern for erring members.

A FORGIVING FAMILY

How long does one have to tolerate a brother who continues to sin against him? Is there not some stopping place? Surely if we do not draw a line and cease to forgive, that brother will find us soft and will take advantage of us.

Such must have been Peter's response to Jesus' teaching when he asked, "Lord, how often shall my brother sin against me, and I forgive him? As many as seven times?" (Matt. 18:21). Peter's suggestion sounds very reasonable, if not generous.

But Jesus asked for more. "I do not say to you seven times, but seventy times seven" (Matt. 18:22). That is, there is no limit to the community's capacity to forgive.

Other community may draw limits to such kind-

37

ness; but Jesus' community does not measure out forgiveness as if there were only a limited amount. Where there is repentance, this community sets no limit on forgiveness.

That Jesus intended for his community to be a fellowship of forgiveness is demonstrated in the parable which follows Jesus' dialogue with Peter. "The kingdom of heaven may be compared to a king who wished to settle accounts with his servants," said Jesus (Matt. 18:23). The story gives us another clue into the nature of the kingdom. And as the message of the story demonstrates, this kingdom is not like any other institution.

We are told that the king had a servant who owed him ten thousand talents. We miss the whole point of the story if we do not recognize the importance of the sum. The highest denomination of currency was the talent; and ten thousand talents was an astronomical sume which no one could pay (roughly ten million dollars).

Jesus thus tells a story about a man who owed a sum which could not have been repaid in several lifetimes. He could only plead for mercy. The story was shocking to Jesus' listeners because the man did indeed receive mercy, being released from a debt he could never have paid.

Such a story is a reminder of the nature of the kingdom of God. In the kingdom of God each of us stands before the king who has released us from an enormous debt.

But the story does not end with the servant's good fortune. We are told that immediately after he was released from his debt he encountered someone who owed him the trifling sum of 100 denarii (about twenty dollars). The contrast is between the two servants and the two sums of money. The very servant who had been released from his debt now had his debtor thrown into prison for nonpayment of a very small sum. The one who had received mercy was not willing to be merciful! Because of his behavior the king became angry and cast this unmerciful debtor into prison.

What does this story tell us about the community of Jesus? The point is that each of us stands in the identical place of this unmerciful servant: halfway between God and our brother. Or, to put it another way, each of us stands between the forgiveness that is granted us and the forgiveness that is asked of us. The point was made already in the Lord's model prayer: "Forgive us our debts as we also have forgiven our debtors" (Matt. 6:12).

The Christian family is bound together by the adhesive of mutual service.

In the Christian community there should be a capacity for forgiveness that is not found in other institutions, for the Christian is motivated by the forgiveness he has received. When we live by the forgiveness we have received, the offenses of our brother can only appear trivial.

Perhaps it is the experience of being forgiven that allows the Christian community to see the offenses of others in perspective. It is easy to allow our brother's offense against us to take on a significance that it should not have. Many communities break down precisely at this point because they have no way to respond to the tensions which inevitably arise. But the Christian community is unlike other communities, for it has learned from Jesus Christ the meaning of forgiveness.

BOUND TOGETHER BY SERVICE

It was natural that the disciples would have expected this new fellowship to function like any other community. What community does not live within a hierarchy of rank and power? In every human community, from the military organization to the civic club, the organization is held together by rank and power. To succeed is to climb to the top of the organization.

This fact allows us to understand why Jesus' disciples had a difficult time grasping the nature of the new community. On one instance we are told, "And an argument arose among them as to which of them was the greatest" (Luke 9:46; cf. 22:24). On another occasion two of the disciples, James and John, came to Jesus asking for the two most important positions in Jesus' kingdom (Mark 10:35-45). The disciples knew of no other way of living in the community that by the rule of rank and power.

Has the church, like the disciples, also lived by the world's standard? Is there within the church at times this same desire for prestige and influence that exists in any human institution?

There is always the temptation to treat public positions of leadership in the church as positions of authority and power. We can be tempted to regard all such positions according to the analogy of business and professional organizations. The minister too easily becomes executive director of the corporation.

Elders and deacons are thought of as the board of directors. We no doubt share the disciples' temptation to ask, "Who shall be greatest?"

"But," said Jesus, "you are not to be like that" (Luke 22:26, NIV). "The kings of the Gentiles exercise lordship over them" (Luke 22:25), but the community of Jesus lives by a different standard. It does not imitate human institutions. "Rather let the greatest among you become as the youngest, and the leader as one who serves" (Luke 22:26).

The community of Jesus does not exist in the same way that the corporation and the military organization exist. The community is not held together by force. Its leaders are not ashamed to "become like children" (Matt. 18:3-4) and to serve one another.

When Jesus encouraged his disciples to live as servants, he dignified a word that in the popular speech of the time never connoted dignity or rank. The servant (*diakonos*) signified self-abasement and humility: waiting at table and serving food.

The distinction between master and servant was nowhere more obvious in the ancient world than at meals. The noble masters would lie at the table in their long robes, while the servants had to wait on them. The word *servant* never lost its flavor of inferiority. Dignity was to be found in the exercise of power.

When Jesus spoke of servanthood as the disciples' ideal, he both dignified a term which was in disrepute and gave a new standard of life for his community. His family does not live by the autocratic power of despots. It lives by the voluntary service of members for each other.

Hans Kung, in *The Church*, has observed that the

early church was determined not to live by the world's standards of power and authority so much so, in fact, that it sysematically excluded from its vocabulary any words which suggested a hierarchy or power.

The word used most frequently for "office" in the early church is *diakonia*—translated usually be *ministry* or *service*. The term is related to *diakonos*, the word for service at the table. The major concern of *diakonia*, ministry, is living for others (Mark 9:35; 10:43-45). Thus, when the early church chose a term to describe those with responsibility in the community, it did not speak of power; it spoke of service for others. Such a style of life was radically different from any human community. The Christian family is bound together by the adhesive of mutual service.

JESUS AS THE MODEL

Why has the church taken this *diakonia* as the foundation of its community life? And why has it resisted so firmly the notions of authority and power? It is because Jesus is our model for leadership.

To those who chose to argue about rank and power, Jesus pointed out that he came as a servant for others (cf. Mark 10:45). The gospel of John portrays this notion graphically with the story of Jesus' activity in washing the feet of the disciples (John 13). Later Paul recalls Jesus as the one who did not "count equality with God a thing to be grasped" and as one who "took on the form of a servant" (Phil. 2:6ff.).

From the beginning of its existence, the Christian community has cherished service for others as an

42

ideal because that is what Jesus taught and practiced. Other communities may live by rank and privilege, but not Christ's church. It lives by mutual service!

To be sure, we have not always lived up to the model which Jesus provided. Often we can see ourselves in the immature disciples' question about rank and power. But then we are overwhelmed once more by the fact that we have been the recipients of the marvelous service of Jesus Christ. That fact leads us to serve others, and thus to form a community modeled after the servanthood of Jesus Christ.

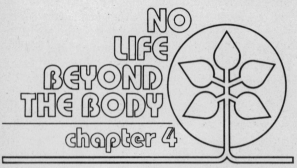

NO LIFE BEYOND THE BODY
chapter 4

"If one member suffers, all suffer together."

1 Corinthians 12:26

Most of the communities to which we belong are voluntary organizations. Because we share a common interest with others, we join with them in forming a community based on that common interest. If we have children in school, we may join with others in forming a chapter of P.T.A. If we are in business, we may join with others who share this particular interest.

Our association with the group lasts as long as we share a common interest with it. When our situation changes, causing us no longer to share common goals with the group, our loyalty to it is likely to disappear. We enter voluntarily and leave voluntarily, because our loyalty and support depend on our sharing common interests with the group.

We need only to take a cursory look at some texts of the New Testament to see that the church is quite unlike the voluntary association. When the New Testament speaks of the community, it has a rich and suggestive word in Greek for developing this idea. It is the word *koinonia,* which we translate as "fellowship" or "participation" or even "partnership." The verb form *koinoneo* can best be translated "to share in." A slightly different form of the word is used when we are told that early Christians had "all things in common" (Acts 2:44; 4:32).

Koinonia is used not only for the human community. It is also frequently used for the Christian's relationship to his Lord. And it is precisely at this point that the Christian fellowship is different from all voluntary associations.

The church is not a voluntary association of like-minded people. It is a community of people who have first been called into fellowship with Jesus Christ. We belong to each other because we first belong to Jesus Christ.

MADE PARTNERS BY GRACE

The New Testament will not allow us to forget that we have been made partners with Jesus Christ. Fellowship did not originate at our own initiative. Before there was ever a fellowship, he "partook" of our nature (Heb. 2:14) and shared our situation. Now, as a result, God has "called us into the fellowship of his Son" (1 Cor. 1:9). That is, we have been made partners with Jesus Christ.

Our fellowship with him is not the result of our own goodness. It is his gracious summons that has made us his partners.

Our *partnership* with Jesus Christ is a common theme in the New Testament. Indeed, Paul says in 1 Corinthians 10:16 that the Lord's Supper is a *participation* in the body and blood of the Lord. That is, in the Lord's Supper we recall that we have been summoned into a common life with Jesus Christ. He has made us his partners in salvation. Therefore, we are reminded at the Lord's Supper of our unity with Christ.

In the Lord's Supper we recall that we have been summoned into a common life with Jesus Christ.

But what does it mean to experience fellowship with Christ? Paul spells this idea out more fully in Philippians 3:10 when he speaks of his desire to know "the fellowship of his sufferings." That is, to have fellowship with Christ is to take up his kind of life and even to share his cross. Thus, Paul can describe himself as one who has been "crucified with Christ" (Gal. 2:20). To be a disciple is to share in Jesus' death (Rom. 6:8), his sufferings (2 Cor. 1:5-7; 4:10f.), and even in his weakness (2 Cor. 13:4; cf. Gal. 6:17).

When Paul speaks of fellowship with Christ, he is using no vague generality. Jesus Christ has called his people into a life of sharing his way, the way of the cross. To be in fellowship with Christ is to adopt his kind of life.

This strong emphasis on fellowship with Christ allows us to see the distinction between the church and the voluntary organization. The church is not an organization formed to promote a common interest. It is composed of those people who have been summoned into a common life with Jesus Christ. Because we have a common life with Christ, we have a common life with each other.

FELLOWSHIP IN HIS BODY AND BLOOD

Christianity means community through and in Jesus Christ. We belong to each other only through him. This connection between fellowship with Christ and fellowship with our brother is explicitly spelled out in Paul's description of what happens at the Lord's Supper. It is in the very act of sharing in Christ's body and blood that we are brought together as one body (1 Cor. 10:16, 17). We are thus brought together when we share him.

A similar idea is suggested in 1 Corinthians 12:12 when Paul says, "For just as the body is one and has many members, and all the members of the body, though many, are one body, so it is with Christ." The analogy suggests that Christ is the one body, and that there are many who share in him. The various members of the church, each with his own gift, comprise the very body of Christ. Because we share in him, we are a fellowship of partners.

There is always the danger that the partnership will break apart into smaller units. Indeed, the problem which Paul addresses in Corinth seems to be the result of members who thought they could continue the Christian life without a partnership. However, Paul's description of the church as the body of Christ provides an excellent opportunity for him to demonstrate how the church is to make its partnership real.

The Corinthians behaved as if some parts of the

47

body were quite dispensable, while other parts could exist in isolation from the community (1 Cor. 12:15-22).

The problem at Corinth was that the Christians were so centered on fellowship with Christ alone that fellowship with the church no longer mattered. Those who spoke in tongues were willing to talk to God and edify themselves at the expense of the rest of the church (1 Cor. 14:4). Thus the partnership at Corinth had given way to *individualism*. The church had been broken into various parts.

Against the background of those Corinthian individualists Paul argues that the church is actually Christ's body. There is no relationship to Christ apart from the body because each of us is only a partner in Jesus Christ (1 Cor. 12:12). He is the body, and all of us are merely parts of that body. Even those parts of the body which seem insignificant are really indispensable (1 Cor. 12:22). We are not merely baptized into Christ; we are baptized "into his body" (1 Cor. 12:13). Thus, *fellowship with Christ necessitates fellowship with his body.*

NO LIFE OUTSIDE THE BODY

Have we taken seriously the implications of Paul's description of the body of Christ? Paul's reflections should have an impact on our functioning as Christian people. Not only is our community created by Christ, but also there is no relationship to Jesus Christ without our being members of his body, the church! And fellowship is real only when every one of us, like parts of a body, contributes to the ongoing ministry. Even those members who seem not very gifted are vital to the fellowship, for the body cannot

48

exist without the cooperation of its tiniest part.

Fellowship is never a reality unless the work is shared by all members. Even where the church is blessed with an excellent professional team of ministers, there is no justification for a ministry carried out by staff members alone. To limit ministry to the work of a few individuals is to violate Paul's argument about the church as a body composed of interdependent members.

Christians within the body are not spectators to the work of the church. Nor is their work simply that of financial benefactors. As parts of the body, they are actively engaged in the ongoing work of Christ. One part of the body may be especially gifted in the church's benevolent ministry, while another is gifted in his liberality, and another is a capable teacher (Rom. 12:6). Together, with our shared responsibilities, we function as Christ's body. Unless we share this task, the fellowship is destroyed, for the members of Christ's body are, like the parts of the human body, interdependent.

MEMBERS ONE OF ANOTHER

Paul carries the language of the body of Christ further when he says, "If one member suffers all suffer together; if one member is honored, all rejoice together" (1 Cor. 12:26). It is absurd to think of isolating pain to one part of the human body, for there is a *sympathy* which unites our members. It is no less true of Christ's body, the church. We are bound together by this sympathy.

"No man is an island" in the church, for we share common life. We are so much a part of the common life that we cannot be apathetic toward the misfortunes of a brother.

The human tragedy that strikes one member reverberates throughout the whole church. It is seen in the church's intercessory prayers for each other and its willingness to sacrifice to help a member who suffers. This spirit has been seen in many instances where Christians have made financial contributions on behalf of others in the church. Elsewhere it has been seen in the unselfish way members have given their time to help a suffering member of the body.

Fellowship with Christ necessitates fellowship with his body.

E. R. Dodds attempts to tell us why Christianity triumphed in the ancient world. His answer concerns these bonds of sympathy that were to be found in the early church:

. . . (it) was from the first a community in a much fuller sense than any corresponding group . . . . Its members were bound together not only by common rites, but by a common way of life and . . . by their common danger. Their promptitude in bringing material help to brethren in captivity or other distress is attested not only by Christian writers, but by Lucian, a far from sympathetic witness. Love of one's neighbor is not an exclusively Christian virtue, but in our period the Christians seem to have practiced it more effectively than any other group. The church provided the essentials of social security: it cared for widows and orphans, the old, the unemployed, and the disabled.[1]

Dodds goes on to say that the church provided something more than material benefits. It was the "sense of belonging" which the Christian community provided. Rootless people in the great cities needed to belong somewhere. There were the newly freed slaves, the new immigrants to the city, the peasant who had come to town in search of work. For people in this situation, membership in the body of Christ might be the only way of maintaining their sense of identity and giving their life some semblance of meaning. It was because Christians were "members of one another," concludes Dodds, that Christianity spread as it did. This sense of sympathy, which Paul describes in 1 Corinthians 12:26, answers a human need.

Is our situation really different from that which the early Christians faced? Because of the widespread mobility in our culture, there are many, many people who are looking for a place where the suffering of one is shared by others.

For Paul the church was the one place where genuine sympathy was to be found. The church dare not be less today.

PARTNERS IN A SHARED TASK

The New Testament indicates that fellowship (*koinonia*) is far more than sharing the benefits of salvation. Fellowship also involves what we do together as partners (*koinonoi*) in a common task. This term "partner" is very appropriately used for our relationship to each other.

It is used in Luke 5:10, where we are told that James and John were partners in a business relationship. Certainly, as partners, they were colleagues

51

who shared a common task and were engaged in the same trade. Their partnership may have involved a specified work routine and a division of labor. Perhaps they shared expenses as well as benefits. Partnership involved a shared task.

This word *koinonos,* used in Luke 5:10 for a business partnership, is an important word for the relationship of disciples to each other. Paul describes Titus as a partner and fellow laborer (2 Cor. 8:23). Their work as missionaries was nothing less than a partnership in Christ's service. When Paul appeals to Philemon to accept Onesimus, the runaway slave, he appeals with the words, "If you consider me your partner, receive him as you would receive me" (Philem. 17). Paul's appeal rests not on coercion and power; it rests on Philemon's acknowledgment that he is Paul's partner in the faith.

To have fellowship with Christ is to take up his kind of life and even to share his cross.

Our New Testament texts demonstrate that this partnership is never a passive matter. Partnership is made concrete in deeds. Thus, the financial assistance of the Philippian church leads Paul to thank them for their "partnership in the gospel" (Phil. 1:5). The author of Hebrews recalls that his readers in earlier days had been partners with other Christians who had suffered abuse (Heb. 10:33).

In another context, we are told that Paul's mission among Gentiles had led Jewish Christians to distrust him until they became aware that God's grace had been given to Paul for this work. It was only then that they gave to Paul "the right hand of fellowship" (Gal. 2:9); i.e., they recognized him as a partner in a common task.

These references indicate that partnership can involve a shared task, financial support, or even shared sufferings. Only when partnership is concretely realized in such experiences can fellowship be real.

AUTHENTIC CHRISTIAN FELLOWSHIP

Have we taken seriously the fact that Christ has made us partners in a shared task? The notion of partnership excludes the common idea that the church can ever be a *they* which is separate from the life and work of the members.

Partnership means joint participation of all members. It implies that no part of the church—including the professional ministry and the leadership—can ever become removed from the rest of the church. For partnership involves mutual giving and receiving. Even those who proclaim the word or administer the church's affairs are only exercising one gift among many (1 Cor. 12:28). Partnership is real when all members are actively involved in the task to which Christ has summoned us. This is Christian fellowship.

When we take this notion of partnership seriously, we begin to look upon the very diversity of the church as a blessing. The one Lord is active in making one body from our diversity. It is important that no one be merely a passive participant in the partnership. We fail to realize this partnership whenever we exclude any segment of the church from the partnership of service.

There has been a tendency in some instances to assume that the youth and the elderly are only passive recipients within the partnership. But when we fail to allow a place for the contribution of either, we fail to take them seriously as our equals in the partnership of service. There are unique contributions to the community which only the youth group can make. Similarly, there are contributions which can be made by the elderly, by the widows of the church, or by young families.

Partnership breaks down when the work is done by only one segment of the church. No doubt we will find our church life healthier when we provide a task of service for each person in the church. It is when we allow everyone to assume a task that we show we take them seriously as vital parts of the community.

The church is a community, but it is not like human communities. For the fellowship of the church is not a human creation. We exist together in this partnership because Christ has brought us together. We are partners with each other because we are partners with Christ.

1. E. R. Dodds, *Pagan and Christian in an Age of Anxiety* (New York City: Norton, 1970), p. 137.

A GIVING FELLOWSHIP
chapter 5

"And they had all things in common." Acts 2:44

For many people the collection is an intrusion of secular matters into the worship service. For others it is a kind of appendage to the Lord's Supper, a transitional point between the communion service and other moments in the hour of worship.

The church will not be encouraged to give if the collection is only an intrusion of secular affairs into the worship. What the church needs, therefore, is to see those motivations which once led the church to contribute its funds selflessly to the cause of the gospel.

The early church gave because there was from the first a commitment to sharing life together. The opening chapters of Acts portray an idyllic view of the earliest church after Pentecost. They accepted the responsibility of sacrificial giving: "For as many

55

as were possessors of lands or houses sold them, and brought the proceeds of what was sold and laid it at the apostles' feet; and distribution was made to each as any had need" (Acts 4:34b-35).

INFECTIOUS GIVING

We see a story of sacrificial giving. A young man named Barnabas sold a field and brought the money to the apostles (Acts 4:36f.). The spirit of sharing seemed infectious. The infant church was determined to fulfil, by its own actions, the hope of Deuteronomy 15:4, that "there will be no poor among you."

At one point there seemed to be a breakdown in this spirit of sharing, a lapse that was manifest when some of the Grecian widows were neglected (Acts 6:1ff.). But deacons were appointed to remedy this problem.

It is signficant that sacrifice was never demanded by authority. This was *no* legally imposed communism, where the price of admission to the community was the liquidation of one's property.

In this respect the church, which had "all things in common" (Acts 2:44), was different from another group of their time which held property in common. Josephus records of the Essenes:

It is wonderful too how they share everything with each other; one discovers among them none who possesses more than another. For they have a rule that whoever joins the sect must place his property at the disposal of the society for its common use, so that in general one finds neither the degradation of poverty nor the distinction of wealth (*War* ii. 8. 3-4).

56

What Luke describes in the first chapters of Acts is different from the communism of the Essenes. There was no rule compelling Christians to dispose of their goods. What the Essenes did by the compulsion of authority, the Christians did voluntarily.

THE POWER OF FELLOWSHIP

What could motivate the infant church to practice such incredible financial sacrifice? Luke portrays the early church as the community of the new age motivated by the power of the Holy Spirit.

Indeed, their sacrificial giving was only part of the total picture of the fellowship of the church. As a new body called into existence by the preaching of Christ, they now experienced a common life composed of "apostles teaching and fellowship, the breaking of bread and prayers" (Acts. 2:42).

An important part of the new life was "fellowship" (*koinonia*), the sharing of this new life in Christ. These Christians did not stand alone as isolated individuals. Their commitment to Jesus Christ was reinforced by the fellowship of other Christians—the fellowship of worship, of the common meal, and of corporate prayer. The power of this fellowship is seen in Luke's description of the life of the church: "The company of those who believed were of one heart and soul" (Acts 4:32).

This power of fellowship, strengthened in corporate worship and in the regular meals, was the motivating force for sacrificial giving by the Jerusalem church. Their giving was a spontaneous response to the love expressed by Christ and the Spirit.

In the same way, our giving is not a secular matter,

a mere nuisance in the religious life. It is a part of our new life of sharing.

When Luke describes the fellowship of the infant church, he uses the Greek word *koinonia* to describe the common life. When he describes the financial sacrifices of the church, he says on two occasions that they had "all things in common" (2:44; 4:32), using the related word *koinos*. For this ideal church described by Luke, giving was a shared act, a part of the life of fellowship. When we are able to see giving as a part of our life together we will have discovered the motivation to give.

The early church realized that the life of fellowship could never be attained as long as there were economic barriers separating the people. There could be no common life of prayer and worship without a common caring for the needs of the less fortunate. Thus, fellowship to the earliest church meant far more than friendship between peers. Fellowship involved the common life where economic barriers were crossed and the needy were cared for by the community. Fellowship was not just a word; it took concrete form in the act of giving.

FELLOWSHIP IN ACTION

The religious significance which the Jerusalem church attached to giving was not forgotten in the works of Paul. He was deeply involved in a matter of considerable financial importance. Paul played the role of the minister whose task was to urge his people to give. But what significance did giving have for Paul? His epistles provide an answer.

There are scattered references in Paul's epistles and in Acts to a collection which had extreme importance for Paul. Acts 11:29 refers to a collection in Gentile areas for the benefit of the churches in Judea. This ministry was carried out by Paul and Barnabas (12:25; 24:17).

Undoubtedly, the standard of living in the great cities of Antioch and Corinth was far greater than in Palestine. Indeed, this collection on behalf of the Judean churches was reminiscent of those collections which synagogues in cities like Antioch frequently sent to Jerusalem. Giving for the relief of others was, as Luke says, "a ministry" (Acts 11:29; 12:25).

Their giving was a spontaneous response to the love expressed by Christ and the Spirit.

When we get to Paul's personal comments on the collection we see how vital a place it had in his work. It becomes apparent at the beginning of the Gentile ministry. The leaders of the Jerusalem church were disturbed when they heard the reports of the success of the Gentile mission. This success could produce radical changes in the composition of the church.

Paul recalls in the second chapter of Galatians that, after fourteen years of missionary labor, he went to Jerusalem to discuss his work among the leaders of the Jerusalem church. As the leader of the Gentile churches, Paul did not know what to expect from the Jewish leaders. To his relief, James and Cephas and John, the pillars of the Jerusalem church, offered Paul and Barnabas "the right hand of fellowship" (Gal. 2:9).

This shaking of hands was an expression of the full fellowship established by faith in Jesus Christ. The Jewish Christians acknowledged that both they and Paul were sharing in a common work as companions in the gospel. Despite any possible barriers, they had found fellowship in Christ.

Fellowship was, however, more than an empty word. There was a stipulation involved in this fellowship: the Gentile churches were to "remember the poor" (Gal. 2:10). Fellowship was never real until it was expressed in concrete acts of sacrifice.

The giving of money by the Gentile churches was not a matter of finances alone; it was a way of strengthening ties of fellowship. It expressed at the deepest level the fellowship between the original Jewish Christians and the Gentile missionary congregations. Thus, the collection had an important religious significance.

FELLOWSHIP AS A GIFT

Throughout the years of Paul's labors, he did not forget his original agreement with the Palestinian churches. He indicates in 1 Corinthians 16:1 that it was his common practice to request that the collection be made for the Jerusalem Christians. Apparently Paul had instructed the Corinthian church previously about the importance of the collection. Here he replies to questions which the Corinthian church had raised on that subject. The collection for the saints was of vital importance in Paul's teaching.

When Paul speaks of the collection he never employs terms that are merely technical fiscal terms. The word "contribution" (*logeia*) in 1 Corinthians 16:1 was a regular term for sacred collections on

60

behalf of the gods. The collection for the saints was, therefore, a religious matter, a service to God.

The other terms which Paul uses in the New Testament for the collection are likewise words which have their place in devotional usage. Such terms depict acts of love. Thus the collection is called a "gift" (1 Cor. 16:3; 2 Cor. 8:4f.). This word, *charis*, is regularly translated grace and used for the grace of God (Eph. 2:8). Similarly, the collection is called a "blessing" (*eulogia*), a term which is used for the spiritual blessings in Jesus Christ (2 Cor. 9:5; cf. Gal. 3:14; Eph. 1:3).

It was as if Paul had said, in encouraging Christians to share in the collection, "God has richly given you his gift and his blessing in Jesus Christ; now you are summoned, through your financial support, to bring blessings and gifts to others." The collection, far from being a secular matter, was a way of responding to God's grace.

SHARING A COMMON TASK

No term was more expressive of the religious significance of the collection than the word "fellowship" (*koinonia*). We have already seen this term in Galatians 2:9-10 in connection with the collection. It was an especially appropriate term for Paul, for it is used throughout the New Testament for the unity of believers created by Jesus Christ (1 Cor. 10:16f.).

Paul knew that believers are brought into fellowship in the Lord's Supper and that the allegiance to the same Lord knocks down all human barriers. In the same way, the sharing in the common task of giving also creates unity and fellowship.

It is for this reason that Paul speaks of the Macedonians who "gave according to their means . . . begging us earnestly for the favor of taking part in the relief of the saints" (2 Cor. 8:4). The collection is a "taking part," a fellowship (*koinonia*) in a common task.

That the collection is a means of expressing fellowship in the church is also suggested in 2 Corinthians 9:13. Paul there encourages his readers to show "the generosity of your contribution for them and for all others." Those who were to receive the contribution were the Jewish churches. But once more, in Paul's terminology, it was more than a contribution. It was a "fellowship" to which he summoned the Corinthian church, for *koinonia* is again the term which Paul uses for the contribution.

There was something far more important than the amount of money taken up in the contribution. What was of primary importance was the fellowship between Jewish and Gentile Christians expressed in the collection. The contribution was a means of sharing with the Jerusalem church. It was a test of how willing the Gentile church was to embrace those Jewish Christians who had only begun to accept them as brothers.

We cannot overlook the symbolic significance which the collection held in Paul's thinking for bringing the Jewish and Gentile churches together. Paul knew of the tensions which threatened to divide the Jewish and Gentile churches. He wanted some means of holding the churches together. The collection was of enormous importance for this task.

Many years had passed since he had begun to take up the collection for the Jerusalem church. Yet Paul was still involved in the task.

Paul was not certain that his mission would be successful, and he asked for the prayers of the Roman church "that my service for Jerusalem may be acceptable to the saints" (Rom. 15:31). He tells the Roman readers how the Philippian and Achaian churches had voluntarily shared in this contribution, or "fellowship" (*koinonia*). "And indeed," he adds, "they are in debt to them, for if the Gentiles have come to share in their spiritual blessings, they ought also to be of service to them in material blessings" (Rom. 15:26-27).

The word for "share" is *koinoneo*. Fellowship is expressed, not by mere word, but by sharing in the act of giving. The collection carried with it the memory that the Jerusalem churches had once shared spiritual blessings, creating a fellowship. Now the church could join hands across the Mediterranean and make fellowship real by sharing its material blessings.

A sacrifice demanded of an individual is often ineffectual if he cannot see that he is sharing a common task with others. Few Americans make sacrifices for their country if they must make them alone. But where a commitment is shared by others, sacrifices can be effective. Similarly, Christians are capable of extraordinary sacrifices where there is a sharing, or fellowship, of giving. Indeed, a people may be brought together in greater harmony by a shared sacrifice.

Perhaps this is the reason why one of Paul's favorite terms for the collection is "fellowship." The collection for a common task makes concrete the unity to which Christ has called us.

PARTNERS IN THE GOSPEL

It was not only in the important task of bringing the Jewish and Gentile churches into harmony that Paul saw the collection as a way of establishing fellowship. There was, for Paul, an important principle that the one who "is taught the word" should share (*koinoneo*) all good things with him who teaches" (Gal. 6:6).

The preacher and the hearer are "partners" in fellowship, each doing his part to strengthen the Christian community. The proclaimer shares his life and message with the hearers; the hearers share their material blessings, thus entering into fellowship through giving.

No community exemplified this spirit of fellowship more totally than the Philippian church. When Paul writes to this church, he mentions at the first of the epistle his appreciation for their "partnership in the gospel" (Phil. 1:5). Christ had created between Paul and this community a "fellowship" (*koinonia*), or common life. Only in the letter to the Philippians does Paul make special mention of the *participation,* or *fellowship*, which he enjoyed with the readers.

Undoubtedly it was the behavior of this church which prompted Paul to mention their partnership with him. He did not forget their financial support in earlier days: "No church entered into partnership with me in giving and receiving except you only; for even in Thessalonica you sent me help once and again" (Phil. 4:15). The word rendered "entered into partnership" is *koinoneo*. Thus Paul's statement can be understood, "No one fellowshipped me . . . except you only."

Financial support was for Paul a sharing in a common task. It was a demonstration that the fellowship established by Christ between Christians was real.

When the church gives to support the preaching of the gospel, its members strengthen the ties of fellowship which come from a shared task. But the fellowship of giving does not end here.

Paul shared with the original church in Jerusalem the view that there could be no real unity as long as brethren were divided along economic lines. Thus, there is a fellowship of giving where the collection is used to help the disadvantaged. When Paul says, "Contribute to the needs of the saints" (Rom. 12:13), he is using the verb *koinoneo*. His counsel might be paraphrased, "Practice fellowship by helping the needy."

The author of Hebrews gives similar advice to his readers when he says, "Do not neglect to do good and to share what you have, for such sacrifices are pleasing to God" (Heb. 13:16). No church can be brought to share spiritual blessings unless there is also a sharing of material blessings.

We need to learn some lessons from the early church's view of giving. In many instances we may be too far removed from the actual disbursement of funds to recognize that we are sharing in a common task with others. Or, there may not be adequate communication within a church to give us an understanding of the fellowship of giving. But where the body of believers can see their giving not as a private task but as a shared task, today's church can enjoy the results of the fellowship of giving.

THE SECRET OF THE SUPPER

chapter 6

"The cup of blessing . . . is it not the communion of the blood of Christ."

1 Corinthians 10:16, KJV

Like a curious child, the visitor who attends the worship service for the first time wonders about the meaning of the loaf and cup shared by the congregation. If he were to ask for an explanation of this custom, he might be told that this service is a memorial to the death of Jesus. He also might be told, in the words of 1 Corinthians 11:26, that the church is "proclaiming the Lord's death until he comes." He might be told that this is simply "the communion."

But what do we mean when we refer to the Lord's Supper as the communion? Does this term refer to a private communion with God—communion in which each Christian is sealed off from his brother or sister in Christ in order to enjoy his own private experiences with God? Or does the term refer to a communion with fellow Christians in which the church is brought closer together in unity?

It was Paul who first referred to the Lord's Supper as a *communion* (1 Cor. 10:16, KJV). He used this term at a time when the Lord's Supper had been turned into chaos. The Corinthians had so destroyed the meaning of the Lord's Supper that Paul dared to say, "When you meet together, it is not the Lord's Supper that you eat" (1 Cor. 11:20). Paul attempted to correct this church's distortion of the Lord's Supper by pleading, "The cup of blessing which we bless, is it not the communion of the blood of Christ? The bread which we break, is it not the communion of the body of Christ?" (1 Cor. 10:16, KJV).

If the Corinthian church had not distorted the Lord's Supper, we might never have been privileged to have Paul's teaching on the subject. When Paul was challenged to teach the Corinthians the real meaning of the Lord's Supper, he taught them that it was a *communion*. We must look further into the problem at Corinth in order to grasp more fully what this term meant for Paul.

DESPISING GOD'S CHILDREN

Paul was convinced that the Corinthians had forgotten the Lord's Supper is a communion. Their problem apparently was *not* in refusing to take the Lord's Supper seriously. The Lord's Supper was neither omitted in the Corinthian church nor taken lightly. Paul's rebuke to the Corinthian Christians suggests that their problem had resulted from a false understanding of the Lord's Supper.

What had happened to the Lord's Supper at

Corinth? A system of cliques and splits came to light when the congregation was gathered. Indeed, the situation was so severe that Paul says, "I do not commend you, because when you come together it is not for the better but for the worse" (1 Cor. 11:17).

When the church assembled, there were "divisions" (*schismata*) which threatened to destroy the church. These were not divisions over false teaching or over the party spirit that had been mentioned previously (1 Cor. 11:20ff.). Nevertheless they were divisions that threatened to destroy the Lord's Supper.

The Lord's Supper is more than a vertical communion with God.

We get a firm understanding of the insidious nature of these divisions when Paul says, "When you meet together, it is not the Lord's Supper that you eat. For in eating, each one goes ahead with his own meal, and one is hungry and another is drunk" (1 Cor. 11:20-21). The problem was that while some of the Christians feasted, others were hungry and were forced to feel their poverty painfully and shamefully.

The Corinthian congregation, which should have been a company of brothers and sisters at worship, presented a shameless picture of social division. As Paul says, "Or do you despise the church of God and humiliate those who have nothing?" (1 Cor. 11:22).

It was the purpose of the gospel to establish peace among brethren; but at Corinth the brethren were divided along social and economic lines. Paul saw a church divided into the categories of rich and poor at the Lord's Supper, and he knew that what they shared was not "the Lord's Supper" (1 Cor. 11:20). Christ is the Lord of unity, and not of division.

Paul's concern with healing the social divisions in the church was manifested in a later exhortation. He says, "So then, my brethren, when you come together to eat, wait for one another" (1 Cor. 11:33). The poorer Christians had no day off from work. Sunday was not a holiday. Apparently the wealthier Christians did not bother to wait for their poorer brethren, thus intensifying the social division in the church.

The Lord's Supper at Corinth was far from being a communion of brothers and sisters with each other. It had become an occasion for cliques to separate brethren. Wherever that happens the Supper is distorted.

JUST YOU AND ME, GOD

How could such an occasion have arisen? A reading of 1 Corinthians does not indicate that the Christians in that city consciously abused the Lord's Supper. Their fault was the result of a misunderstanding of the feast. They took the Lord's Supper with total seriousness. But if one had asked them what the Lord's Supper meant, they might have replied that it was a private communion with God.

It is even likely that the Corinthian Christians thought there was something magical in the elements themselves. They may have believed that the mere partaking of the communion was a guarantee of eternal salvation. Consequently they may have thought they could partake of the Lord's Supper without caring for their brother because it was purely a matter between themselves and God!

This kind of teaching seems to be the background of Paul's warning in 1 Corinthians 10:1-13. It was to people who recalled that their forefathers had been saved in the wilderness by eating and drinking "supernatural food" (10:3) that Paul gave a lesson from the Old Testament. The lesson was simple: the fact that the wilderness generation had eaten "supernatural food" and had drunk "supernatural drink" did not guarantee their salvation (10:3, 4). Even most of those who had partaken of the supernatural food were "overthrown in the wilderness" (10:5). This lesson from history served to warn the Corinthians that salvation is never guaranteed simply from eating "supernatural food" and drinking "supernatural drink."

Paul's warning is a reminder for today's church. One may take the Lord's Supper with total seriousness; he may be faithful in his participation. But if he neglects his brother and forgets the rest of the community, it is not the Lord's Supper at all (1 Cor. 11:20).

The Lord's Supper is more than a vertical communion with God. It is also a time when Christians recall the intimate relationships with their brothers and sisters.

THIS IS MY BODY

As we have seen, the chaos at Corinth occasioned Paul's teaching on the Lord's Supper. In 1 Corinthians 11:23-26 Paul reminds his readers of the origin of the Lord's Supper "on the night when he was betrayed." He recalls that he had originally taught them this story, and that he had received it "from the Lord." It is as if the apostle were saying, "Don't you

70

recall what I taught you originally? And don't you see the implications of what you were taught?"

The exclusive one-to-one relationship to God manifest among Christians at Corinth was, to Paul, a corruption of Jesus' words, "This is my body" and "this is my blood." These words of Jesus remind the church of the real meaning of the Lord's Supper.

We are especially fortunate that in 1 Corinthians 10:16-17 we have Paul's own commentary on Jesus' words found in 1 Corinthians 11:23-25. Paul asks, "The cup of blessing which we bless, is it not a participation in the blood of Christ? The bread which we break, is it not a participation in the body of Christ?" When Paul gives his commentary on Jesus' words at the institution of the Lord's Supper, he describes the Lord's Supper as a "participation" in the body and blood of Christ. As the KJV and the ASV put it, the Lord's Supper is a *communion* in the body and blood of Christ. The NEB renders, "a sharing of the blood" and "a sharing of the body of Christ."

MORE THAN A MEMORIAL

But what does Paul mean by *communion* (KJV, ASV) or *participation* (RSV) at the Lord's Supper? Again the Greek word is the term *koinonia,* which has the basic meaning of a sharing of something that is held in common. *Koinonia* is often translated "fellowship." It is the term for an intimate relationship between close companions, as in the Christian's relationship to Jesus Christ.

The Christian at baptism shares in the fate of Jesus—in his death and resurrection (Rom. 6:5ff.). At the Lord's Supper the Christian becomes the

71

intimate companion of Christ, and thus "participates in" his death for us. It is in the Lord's Supper that we share in his death for us. And it is in the Lord's Supper that we share the benefits of salvation.

Communion, then, means "sharing with Christ." In the Lord's Supper Jesus is present with the church. There is indeed a vertical relationship between the believer and his Lord, for in partaking of his body and blood we unite with him and become his companions. The Lord's Supper is far more than a memorial for a deceased Lord. It is a time for communion, for *fellowship* with the One who is still present with the church.

To share in Jesus Christ is to be brought into fellowship with others.

Paul's Corinthian readers might have agreed with him when he spoke of the vertical relationship with Jesus Christ in the Lord's Supper. Nevertheless, there was still something radically wrong with a church which could be so divided at the Lord's Supper. Their problem, apparently, was that they saw themselves as isolated individuals, each communing privately with his Lord. As long as they saw the Lord's Supper in this light, they could ignore their brother in all good conscience.

Private religious experience is no substitute for love among brethren. Paul will not tolerate such an attitude. The Lord's Supper does not divide brothers!

Immediately after Paul reminds his readers that the Lord's Supper is a fellowship or communion in the body and blood of Christ, he adds, "Because there is one bread, we who are many are one body, for we all partake of the one bread" (1 Cor. 10:17). Fellowship with Christ leads to fellowship with Christians, to mutual fellowship with members of the community. One cannot enjoy communion with Christ without also experiencing communion with Christ's body, the church. This is the message which the Corinthians had missed.

Paul concludes that when the church "shares in" Christ's body *the church actually becomes the one body*. The apostle's emphasis is on the unity of the church which is derived from a common origin. There is only "one body" into which the church has been baptized (1 Cor. 12:13). There is only "one body" shared by the church in communion (1 Cor. 10:17). Christians cannot continue to share in the one body of Christ and remain isolated and unloving.

To share in Jesus Christ is to be brought into fellowship with others. By sharing in "the same bread," the church demonstrates in each communion service that it is the unified body of Christ.

This very fact excludes the individualism which characterized worship at Corinth. No one could argue, in the face of Paul's statement, that communion is a private matter between man and God. If in communion we become one body, it is never permissible to disregard members of the community.

DISCERNING THE BODY

Communion has a double focus; it is communion with Christ and communion with other believers. But has not this second feature of communion been largely overlooked? Communion for many people

73

has meant *communion only with God*. Many of the hymns traditionally sung at the Lord's Supper have emphasized only the vertical relationship with God.

Paul never denied that there is a communion with God. However, he also indicated that wherever the Lord's Supper ceases to be a fellowship of Christians, it has been distorted. Every time the church forgets that the Lord's Supper is a fellowship, it agrees more with Paul's opponents than with Paul himself.

The body of Christ has brought us together and made us responsible to one another in love.

We need to understand the situation to which Paul spoke. Then we can appreciate more fully Paul's advice on other matters pertaining to the Lord's Supper. Recalling that the specific offense of the Corinthian church was in the failure of love, Paul's warning about "eating in an unworthy manner" must pertain to behavior that is unloving and an obstacle to fellowship (1 Cor. 11:27).

Those who fail to "discern the body" (1 Cor. 11:29, KJV) are not merely frivolous when they partake of the Lord's Supper; they have disregarded the community, the body of Christ. To "discern the body" is to know that the body of Christ has brought us together and made us responsible to one another in love. As Paul also says: "If one member suffers, all suffer together; if one member is honored, all rejoice together" (1 Cor. 12:26f.). In communion we come together not as isolated members but as parts of the body of Christ.

Sometimes we may wonder if the church will ever learn the lesson which Paul proclaimed to the Corinthian church.

Paul saw in the death of Christ and again in the Lord's Supper a power strong enough to overcome the natural divisions of class and race. The Lord's Supper was to be the demonstration that the dividing wall between groups had broken down into a fellowship created by Christ. Slaves and masters, even Jews and Gentiles, became a fellowship by sharing in the common salvation. No other power seemed capable of tearing down these human barriers. The fellowship of the Lord's Supper was the demonstration of the gospel's power.

Our own world, like Paul's, is tragically divided on the basis of income levels, educational backgrounds, and ethnic origins. If the church is to be true to the Lord whose body was given for all, the Lord's Supper must be the time when groups are welded into "one body."

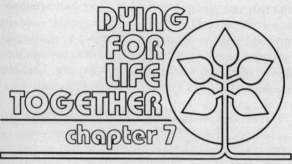

DYING FOR LIFE TOGETHER

chapter 7

"(Love) does not seek its own."

1 Corinthians 13:5, NASB

A popular slogan that appeared several years ago was "do your own thing." No doubt the slogan had a definite appeal, for it was usually understood as a motto calling for freedom and self-expression. It reminded us that our freedom often is curtailed by the opinions and will of others.

If we wanted to be free, we had to "do our own thing." This was the freedom to dress as we wanted, to speak our minds as freely as we wanted, and to live without constant regard for the opinions of others.

Anyone who has lived without this freedom to be himself would naturally find this slogan inviting. It is natural to want to be free.

But even freedom can be distorted and abused.

We have come to understand this in disputes over our civil laws. The call to "do your own thing" can be an excuse for disregarding other people. We can become so wrapped up in our own freedom that we totally disregard the rest of the community.

When personal freedom becomes absolute, chaos results. No one, as Justice Holmes once said, has the right to falsely yell "Fire!" in a crowded theater. Personal freedom must be conditioned by concern for others. The rights of society place limits on our personal freedom. Indeed, there can be no community at all if everyone seeks to please himself without regard for others.

ALL THINGS ARE LAWFUL

This is the issue which Paul confronted when he wrote the first letter to the Corinthians. The church at Corinth had heard Paul's message of freedom in Christ and had taken him seriously! Indeed, it seems likely that the motto of the Corinthian Christians had become, "All things are lawful" (6:12; 10:23).

The problem seems to have been that the Corinthians did not know how to handle their freedom. As a result, the community had begun to fall apart in every aspect of their church life (1 Cor. 1:11; 11:18). The Lord's Supper was a time when rich and poor gathered into cliques. In public worship there was only disorder and chaos (14:26ff.). Some members used the public worship as a forum for demonstrating their gifts (see chapters 12, 14).

Real community life was further hampered because some Christians offended their brothers by eating meat that previously had been offered to idols (1 Cor. 8:9-13). The stronger brother knew this meat

77

was no different from any other. But the weaker brother, who recently had been converted from idolatry, could not shut the pagan associations out of his mind. As an idol worshiper, he had eaten meat in an idol's temple.

Life together in the Corinthian church had come near to falling apart over several issues. Freedom had come to mean "doing your own thing." And this kind of freedom had resulted in chaos.

The community at Corinth had broken down among sincere believers who had been baptized into Christ (1 Cor. 1:13-17; 12:13) and had maintained their Christian commitment. What caused this breakdown of community on so many fronts? It was the fact that for the Corinthians, all things were lawful.

FREE TO IGNORE

Freedom had become the big word at Corinth (1 Cor. 9:1). The Corinthians were sure of their "authority" (8:9). They were so proud of their freedom that some considered themselves free to visit the temple prostitutes (6:13-20). The church was even proud of being free enough to allow one of its members to live in an incestuous relationship (5:1ff.).

This freedom had destroyed the fellowship. The freedom to live without restraint became the freedom to ignore the Christian brother.

The Corinthians never doubted that baptism and the Lord's Supper were descriptive images of a new relationship with God. But they saw this relationship as a private matter between themselves and God. Thus, one could blithely ignore his brother in the Lord's Supper, or offend his conscience, for Christianity was a private matter between the Christian and God.

The Corinthians' doctrine of freedom is still a popular view today. There remain people who apparently believe that they can be isolated Christians. An emphasis on spiritual experience can lead us to believe that faith is only a private matter. Emphasis on personal experience can then lead us to ignore the Christian community.

There is a persistent strain of Corinthian individualism in the church which so emphasizes a personal relationship with Jesus Christ that the life of community is ignored.

Paul will not accept this kind of individualism in the church. To live without restraint, as the Corinthians had done, is not Christian. Thus, Paul devotes a major part of his letter to show that Christianity is lived in community.

To be a Christian is to exercise responsible freedom. It is not the freedom to destroy the community.

EXERCISING FREEDOM RESPONSIBLY

First-century Christians felt the excitement of liberation. Things forbidden in the past now had become permissible. The Corinthian Christians felt the freedom to go to the marketplace where most of the meat offered for sale had once been offered as a sacrifice to a pagan god. "After all," they probably thought, "if we are free, why not use our freedom?"

"We have knowledge," they said (1 Cor. 8:1). They knew that meat was no different from any other meat, and so they were free! But what about the *new* Christian who did not know? Did they have a responsibility to him? The Corinthians chronicled a freedom that ignored the brother.

This is the answer Paul will not accept. "Knowledge puffs up, but love builds up," says Paul (1 Cor. 8:1). Freedom is not absolute! We *are* our brother's keepers. We are even the keepers for those brothers who are unenlightened of the new insights which we have discovered.

Paul instead says, "Not all have this knowledge" (1 Cor. 8:7). He says that this new freedom is a good thing; but it is never an excuse for putting a stumbling block in the way of the weaker brother. This exercise of freedom is never important enough to justify destroying a brother "for whom Christ died" (8:11).

There is *no way* of maintaining a relationship to Jesus Christ without also regarding brothers and sisters in the church. To sin against a brother is to sin against Christ himself (1 Cor. 8:12).

In worship we build up one another—the body of Christ.

It is because the fellowship is important that Paul says, "If food offends my brother, I will never eat meat" (1 Cor. 8:13). To believe in the fellowship is to avoid abusing our freedom.

Some issues are far too trivial to be worth damaging one's relationship to his brother. Our culture is not divided over the issue of vegetarianism. However, we still have issues where we are to restrain our freedom for the sake of another.

There can be no community where freedom is absolute and the feelings of others are ignored. Correctness, according to Paul, is not the only thing that matters, but also love (1 Cor. 8:1). For the sake of love one's dress or his social customs or life-style may reflect a concern for a weaker brother who might be offended. Love compels us to give up "doing our own thing" for the sake of another.

THE LIMITS OF FREEDOM

No human community goes to such lengths to avoid offending a member. We find it striking that Paul can agree in principle with one group and request that their behavior conform to the weaknesses of the other.

Why does Paul place himself in the difficult position of proclaiming freedom while calling on his people to exercise limits on freedom? The answer must come from Paul's understanding of the cross.

His sacrifice was a totally selfless act. Christ died for us. Every brother—even the uninformed brother—is one "for whom Christ died" (1 Cor. 8:11).

Christ died to form his special community. His selfless death is the model for our behavior. If he died for all of us, then our conduct should demonstrate that we live for each other. To live for ourselves at the expense of another is to sin against the cross of Christ.

The cross summons us to give up on the selfish life of unrestrained freedom. It reminds us that Jesus died to bring the community into existence. We too must die daily for the church. There is no Christianity without a community that reflects the meaning of the cross.

ALONE IN THE PEW

The Corinthian Christians were so concerned with their private relationships with God that they had little regard for the community. The spiritual gifts of tongues, prophecy, and knowledge were present in abundance at Corinth. But chaos reigned in the public worship because each was interested in doing his own thing. Apparently everyone wanted to prophesy at the same time (1 Cor. 14:24). And special prestige seems to have accompanied the speaking in tongues, as this was special speech addressed to God (14:2) by which the speaker edified himself (14:4).

There was total confusion at Corinth because each believer was more concerned with his private experience than with the whole community. This perspective is still a common one.

Perhaps one reason why many Christians are so anonymous to each other is that they think of worship as essentially a private experience. The argument that one can feel as close, or closer, to God while alone than while with the church reflects the same individualism. Worship is for many today primarily a private experience.

TO EDIFY THE WHOLE

All public worship must be subjected to one criterion: the principle of deification of the whole community. No private experience, including speaking in tongues, was of value unless it benefited the community. Tongue speaking in Corinth was appropriate only to the extent that the community was edified (1 Cor. 14:27f.; cf. 14:19).

Paul does not deny the validity of the spiritual gifts, for he himself has the gift of tongues (1 Cor. 14:18). The gift of tongues was a way of speaking to God in the Spirit (14:2), and a way of praying (14:13f.). But Paul says that if worship is to be true, it must be comprehensible to all, even the outsider (14:16, 23).

Paul uses the terms *edification* and *edify* in 1 Corinthian 14 no less than seven times. Edification is the goal of all worship. Thus the value of prophecy in Corinthian worship was that the one who prophesied, unlike the tongue speaker, "edified the whole church" (14:4). The gift of tongues was also suitable, provided there was an interpreter who could edify the whole church (14:12-19).

All of this suggests that public worship is, therefore, an act of building up the church. It is here that Christ's community should sense its unity, for Christianity is lived in community.

Does public worship still reflect this desire to edify the whole church? Like the Corinthian community, the church is composed of all kinds of people (cf. 1 Cor. 12:4ff.). How can public worship still edify the entire community?

This desire to edify has to be made manifest in every aspect of worship if we are to live up to Paul's summons. It is important, for instance, that prayers be planned so that they may be the common prayer of the whole body, and not only the private prayer of an individual.

Hymns should also reflect our life together in the church. Some hymns emphasize the first person singular so much that they cease to be the words of a whole body. It is to be expected, moreover, that the musical tastes of the whole body will vary. If the singing of hymns is to edify the whole church, the hymns selected need to express the concerns of each member.

The Corinthians took worship seriously, but their

concern was only with the worship as a means of addressing God. For Paul, worship is more than that. In worship we build up one another—the body of Christ.

THE INDISPENSABLE GIFT

It is worthwhile at this point to show that the great chapter on love, 1 Corinthians 13, falls in the middle of Paul's discussion of public worship. At first glance it appears that Paul has changed the subject. But Paul's chapter on love is an integral part of the entire discussion, for love is God's indispensable gift to this divided community (14:1). For those who argued over the rating of specific gifts, love is "the more excellent way" (12:31).

We have seen the Corinthian church was composed of selfish people who were concerned so much with their own personal devotion that they ignored the community. Already Paul has said that their knowledge is not enough, for it is love which edifies (1 Cor. 8:1). Similarly, he shows in 1 Corinthians 13 that the love which forgets itself in caring for others is indispensable for building the community.

Personal devotion and private religious experience can *never* be a substitute for love. Those who love do not "do their own thing," for love "does not seek its own" (1 Cor. 13:5, NASB). The Christian must learn to seek the good of his neighbor, for that is the lesson of the cross. No community can survive without that love.

AN ACCEPTING FELLOWSHIP

chapter 8

"Welcome one another, therefore, as Christ has welcomed you."

Romans 15:7

How does one establish fellowship in a church where the members come from different cultures and backgrounds? Fellowship does not come automatically.

A church that is uniform in its composition may find it easier to maintain a feeling of community than does a church composed of people from many different backgrounds. A church already united by custom, social class, education, and personal taste may have little problem with fellowship. But a church with a mixed composition may be united only by its common loyalty to Jesus.

Is this common loyalty to Jesus Christ enough to hold the community together without the supporting props of a shared cultural background? We are discovering today, especially in our urban churches, the very problem that was faced in the first generation of Christianity. People who come from widely different backgrounds have different tastes in clothes and music. They come with different customs and habits and even different ideas of right and wrong. One group is likely to adopt more contemporary customs than the other.

Together, in one church, this mixture can be divisive and even explosive. One group is likely to look with disdain at the habits of another. And each group may demand that the others conform to its standards of behavior. In such instances, where different cultures are brought together, the quality of Christian fellowship is tested.

THE TEST OF FELLOWSHIP

It was natural that the first-century church at Rome should face such a problem posed by conflicting cultures. Rome was the greatest city of the empire. Like New York or Paris or London of today, she was a gathering place for many cultures.

Immigrants came here from all parts of the Roman Empire, bringing with them their social customs and traditions. Among these immigrants to Rome were a considerable number of Jews. This wholesale immigration to Rome produced an ethnic diversity in the city which, before long, became reflected within the church. Now, as a result of the church's missionary labors, there were Jews and Gentiles alongside each other in the fellowship.

Under these circumstances could genuine fellowship be maintained? Jewish Christians had a low opinion of Gentile morality (Rom. 1:18-32). And Gentile Christians were inclined to take offense at Jewish spiritual pride.

This problem apparently reached the critical point in Romans 14–15, in the conflict between the *strong* and the *weak* within the church (14:1; 15:1). This conflict, which threatened to destroy the church, was essentially a conflict between two cultures and two life-styles. The strong within the church believed that they could "eat anything," while "the weak man eats only vegetables" (14:2). "One man esteems one day as better than another, while another man esteems all days alike" (14:5). It seems also that one group drank wine while the other did not (14:21).

It is natural for us to assume that God accepts those whom we accept and rejects all whom we reject.

Thus the church at Rome was faced with a division between two cultures which threatened to destroy the fellowship. Already, each group was inclined to despise and pass judgment on the other (Rom. 14:3, 4, 10). Those who had no objections to the eating of meat ignored the feelings of their weaker brother, while the weaker brother sat in judgment on the more liberated brother. The survival of the Christian fellowship in such a situation was given its severest test.

We may think of ourselves as far removed from those cultural divisions of Paul's day. We are no longer divided over the issue of vegetarianism or the observance of special days. But we have replaced them with cultural issues of our day.

Wherever people of different cultures come together, there are problems. We may still wonder if the task of holding the fellowship together is possible in this situation.

SEEING THROUGH GOD'S EYES

The greatest temptation where these differences exist is to assume that God sees only through our eyes. Each cultural group is inclined to think that its standards of behavior and customs are an exact reflection of the mind of God. We want to think that God speaks our language, that he is of our color, and that he shares all of our biases. Thus, it is natural for us to assume that God accepts those whom we accept and rejects all whom we reject.

This attitude was apparently found among the Roman Christians, for each side was busy judging the other (Rom. 14:3). The strong who ate meat as well as the weak who ate only vegetables presumed to stand in God's role as judge.

Paul spoke to both sides in trying to restore the fellowship. "As for the man who is weak in faith, receive him, but not for disputes over opinions" (Rom. 14:1, KJV). These words, addressed to the strong, demanded that they not exclude the less informed brother from the fellowship. The strong might easily have rejected the inconsistencies of the weak, deciding not to regard their consciences.

The strong submit to the weak, not to please themselves, but to edify (Rom. 15:1). Paul finds a "self-pleasing" position untenable from a Christian view. The fellowship is far too important to allow its destruction over these cultural issues.

Although Paul argues in principle for "the strong" (Rom. 14:14), he will *not* tolerate the spirit which is obnoxiously correct. The Christian community, according to Paul, is held together only when we accept in a gracious spirit those brothers whose opinions we consider uniformed.

"Whenever you read the Bible and it makes you self-righteous, you misunderstood it."

Paul seems to place a special burden on the strong, those Christians who are more informed and liberated than their brothers. If in fact they are liberated from the less mature view of "the weak," they have the responsibility not to flaunt their liberation before their weaker brethren.

Few human communities demand such responsibility and discipline from their stronger members. But in the Christian community, such concern for our brother demands that we receive him as he is.

What does it mean to *receive* our weaker brother (Rom. 14:1, KJV)? We must recognize that Paul is demanding more than mere toleration of someone who is a nuisance. What he calls for is a real deference toward those whose views are different.

We have lived for a long time with the tendency to demand that every brother hold the same opinions on everything. If a man is weak in his faith, Paul says you must accept him without attempting to settle matters of opinion (Rom. 14:1). Agreement on all points is not necessary for acceptance into the Christian fellowship, for the quest for Christian unity does not demand uniformity.

Paul does not mean that all opinions are equally true, but that there is room in the church for the weak as well as the strong. Thus, real fellowship exists where we accept those with whom we disagree.

Our congregations still exist with tensions between various groups. There are different age groups, different income levels and different cultures. There are different tastes in worship services; one group wants it highly structured, while another wants it free and spontaneous. Different clothes and hair-styles characterize different life-styles; one group feels itself liberated from tradition while other groups like the security of tradition. The church is big enough for all!

A BURDEN ON THE STRONG

Can the church hold together people who hold nothing in common but mutual allegiance to Jesus Christ? Paul's answer, given to a situation not unlike ours, is that we have a special responsibility to *receive* those who are different from us.

We cannot avoid noticing how much of the burden of holding the fellowship together Paul lays on the strong or enlightened brothers. He seems to be in agreement with them over the question of vegetarianism and the question of drinking wine (Rom. 14:21). But while the strong may be correct in their views, they are not to despise the weaker brother (14:3). Nor are they to place a stumbling block in his path.

There is nothing wrong with eating meat in itself. But even that pleasure is to be renounced if it should

90

cause the stumbling of a brother. "Do not destroy the work of God for the sake of food," says Paul (Rom. 14:20). "It is right not to eat meat or drink wine or do anything that makes your brother stumble" (14:21). Such issues are in fact minor issues, for the "kingdom of God is not eating and drinking" (14:17).

Some freedoms are hardly worth exercising if they destroy our life together. This expression suggests that those who have received higher privileges are obligated to show generosity in their behavior toward those who have been less liberally endowed. So Paul suggests that mature Christians are not interested in scoring points or winning doctrinal arguments against the less informed. They are more concerned with being brothers than with winning arguments.

In many cases being correct on an issue becomes unimportant if our liberation damages our relationship with the rest of the church. A liberated style of dress or a hairstyle or freedom from tradition may be quite defensible. But they also may be minor issues hardly worth damaged relations with a brother. We may paraphrase Paul to say, "The kingdom of God does not consist in length of hair or style of clothes, but in the peace which the spirit provides."

DUTIES FOR THE WEAK

Are there corresponding duties for the weak? If all of the responsibilities for maintaining fellowship were on the strong, we could imagine an unhealthy situation.

The weak and less informed perpetually can hinder the fellowship of the church by persistently objecting to anything new and different. Just as the strong are tempted at times to force their wills on the larger group, the weak may try to force the community to conform to *their* views. They may take the role as God's spokesmen and try to dictate the terms by which the church is held together. That is, unless the whole church submits to their terms there will be no fellowship at all!

The temptation still exists for one segment of the church to demand that all other members conform to their point of view. In some cases they may demand that everyone follow their particular interpretation of scripture. They may assume that everyone who disagrees with their interpretation of scripture is either dishonest or ignorant. Those who persistently define fellowship in narrow terms have in fact presumed to stand as the judges of the faithfulness of others.

Not only the strong have the responsibility of caring for their brother. The word of God cuts both ways! Neither strong nor weak can presume to stand in God's place of judgment. Thus Paul addresses the weak in Romans 14:3-4:

> Let not him who abstains pass judgment on him who eats; for God has welcomed him. Who are you to pass judgment on the servant of another? It is before his own master that he stands or falls.

It is before God that we must one day stand in judgment (Rom. 14:10-12). His word, not ours, ultimately determines the status of our brother before him.

That fact serves as a reminder to any of us who presume to take over God's place of judgment. To assume his role as judge is to destroy the fellowship.

92

To recall that we are fallible creatures whose capacity for judging others is limited, is to make fellowship possible.

One Bible scholar has said, "Whenever you read the Bible and it makes you self-righteous, you misunderstood it." The Bible is never a weapon for scoring points or winning arguments. God's word is a "two-edged sword" which confronts us with our responsibility (Heb. 4:12-13).

Sometimes we are tempted to think that fellowship could become a reality if only the other group were different. If only the others within the church were more tolerant! Or if only they were more enlightened!

Paul's advice in Romans 14–15 reminds both sides of their responsibility to make fellowship possible. Neither group is to "please itself" and neither is to judge the other. The task of weak and strong alike is to "pursue what makes for peace and mutual upbuilding" (14:13, 19; 15:1).

The church is big enough for those who have honest disagreements with us. God has not called us to continue splitting into smaller groups until we all think alike. He has called on us to claim responsibility for maintaining the fellowship which he has created.

WHILE WE WERE YET SINNERS

Paul's advice that we are "not to please ourselves" runs counter to all our natural inclinations. We like to think that fellowship can be real only if our way is pursued. But Paul counsels all of us to forget our selfish demands.

How shall we learn this *selflessness*? Paul's answer is that Christ "did not please himself" (Rom. 15:3). Paul thinks of the cross of Christ, that one great example in which Christ refused to please himself. Instead, he accepted us as we were, long before our behavior deserved his loving act. Christ identified with us "while we were yet sinners" (Rom. 5:8), and brought us into fellowship with him.

Jesus is the one outstanding example of the strong bearing the burdens of the weak. As Paul wrote in Philippians 2:5-8:

Have this mind among yourselves, which is yours in Christ Jesus, who, though he was in the form of God, did not count equality with God a thing to be grasped, but emptied himself, taking the form of a servant, being born in the likeness of men. And being found in human form he humbled himself and became obedient unto death, even death on a cross.

Why should we accept those who disagree with us? Because Christ accepted them. "Receive ye one another, as Christ received you" (Rom. 15:7, KJV).

We can never hold the fellowship together unless we recall that Christ also loved the other side! He is not the Lord only of the culture to which I belong! Thus Paul in Romans 15:7-13 reminds both the strong and the weak that Christ loved the other side. He loved Jews and Gentiles and brought them together. His great desire is that all might "with one voice" glorify God. By coming as a servant to all people, Jesus is the model of the selflesness that holds a fellowship together.

AN ACCEPTING FELLOWSHIP

Few human communities would make the effort

that Paul demands to weld together groups which disagree. Garden clubs, fraternities, and civic clubs are often composed of members who reflect a common background and point of view. But the church as a family must reflect that it serves the Lord who died for all.

At the cross we learn that love is selfless and accepting toward others (Rom. 5:6-11). It becomes our task to be loving toward our brother. To offend him by pleasing ourselves is to fail to love as we are taught. We learn at the cross that even the brother who disagrees with us is "one for whom Christ died."

Jesus never *approved* of immoral behavior or bogus doctrinal positions, yet he demonstrated his *acceptance* on the cross. Because Christ died for everyone, he has given us a new attitude toward our brother who does not share our biases. He has demonstrated his love for both weak and strong by dying to create a fellowship for all.

Can two cultures come together in fellowship? The answer from Romans is not only that we can, but that we are compelled to. The Christ who died for all has created the fellowship. It is maintained when we accept those whom Christ has already accepted.

OUR
LIFE
TOGETHER
chapter 9

"Bear one another's burdens." Galatians 6:2

It is easy to affirm that the gospel is for all. This has been the traditional conviction of the church. Few Christians would dispute the belief that Christ's death was for all, and not for a select few. The problem appears when we ask what this great principle implies for Christian fellowship. Is the principle that Christ died for all an abstract principle which does not concern our life together now? No! The universal gospel must be reflected concretely wherever Christian community gathers.

Our ideal of fellowship is given its severest test wherever the call of the gospel has gone "to all nations" (Matt. 28:19). Are we as a fellowship willing to accept all whom God accepts as a result of the call?

There is an old argument that while we may all be

spiritually one, it is acceptable to exclude from our fellowship those who are different. This proposition was used with greatest enthusiasm to defend the principle of segregation in the churches. It was as if we could be brought together spiritually without ever demonstrating togetherness in a physical way. No doubt this argument has been used to justify other types of segregations. Our natural inclination is to seek out our own kind and open our fellowship only to them.

A GHETTO FELLOWSHIP

This common practice of dividing God's community raises the questions: What kind of fellowship is the church to be? Is it to be a fellowship which reflects the universal call of the gospel? Or is it to be a *ghetto* fellowship where the terms of unity are dictated by one group alone—possibly a minority. A ghetto is by definition a quarter of a city where a minority group lives.

Paul faced the problem of ghetto fellowship when he wrote the Galatian Christians. The success of his missionary work had brought a new problem to the church. Until this time the Jews and Gentiles had been divided by geography. There had been Jewish churches in Judea and Gentile churches in Syria.

What was to happen where the two cultures collide as they did towns like Antioch? Was there to be a Jewish church in one place and a Gentile church elsewhere? Was there to be a church for every different background: one for Asians, one for Africans, and one for Europeans? This was the issue to be decided in the letter to the Galatians.

There were Judaizers in Galatia who had one solution to the problem. They were willing to have fellowship with the Gentiles, but only on their own terms: The Gentiles must become Jews. If not, the Jews certainly would not sit down at the same table for a fellowship meal with Gentiles. Fellowship was defined by one group, the Jews. There were two churches, not one.

THE RIGHT-HANDED CHURCH

The fellowship Paul announced was different from the fellowship which the Judaizers advocated. The apostle recalls that after his successful missionary labors with the Gentiles, the leaders of the Jerusalem church extended to him "the right hand of fellowship (Gal. 2:9)." There were not to be two churches, but one.

The handshake was the sign of a friendly agreement between partners in a common task. Though they worked in different fields, here was the recognition that fellowship is a sharing in a common task. These partners were commissioned for that task by the Lord who gave himself for Jew and Gentile alike.

The "right hand of fellowship" is the church's answer to a difficult problem. It signifies that widely different cultures share a common Lord who can bring them together. It is never enough to have a church divided along ethnic or social lines. Christ dramatically brings us all together and creates a fellowship.

The right words about fellowship come easy, but it is not so easy to make this fellowship come alive. It is not too difficult to express nice sentiments about our brothers in a different country or region. But the ideal of fellowship is severely tested in communities where two cultures come together, as at Antioch. It was there that Jewish and Gentile Christians came side by side in the church.

Antioch was no different from the church in many urban situations today. The city is often the place where people of all backgrounds come together. It is here that fellowship is tested.

PETER'S MISTAKE

Peter found in Antioch that his idea of fellowship was being put to the test. He openly demonstrated Christian fellowship by eating with Gentiles. Sharing a meal for the Jew was the deepest sign of acceptance and brotherhood. Peter's willingness to eat with Gentiles was a bold new step which only the gospel had enabled him to take.

Fellowship was not simply a social gathering for the like-minded. It was a demonstration that God had brought together people of different backgrounds.

Peter made a serious mistake. Under pressure from Judaizers, he ceased to eat with the Gentiles. He "drew back and separated himself, fearing the circumcision party" (Gal. 2:12). The fellowship which Christ had created was now broken. Peter now stood for the principle of two churches instead of one.

Though Peter uttered nice sentiments about fellowship and unity, his actions denied the principle. Paul recoiled as he saw in Peter's life nothing less than hypocrisy.

Paul was so disturbed by Peter's behavior that he "opposed him to his face" (Gal. 2:11). Was Peter's offense merely a breach of social etiquette? No, it was a denial of the entire gospel. Peter's behavior places him in agreement with the Judaizers who would make the Gentiles second-class Christians.

The Jews had no right to claim an advantage with God. As both Paul and Peter had preached, it was not from meritorious keeping of the law that Jews were saved. Salvation was open to all believers, and so no believers could be treated as second class. Peter, in separating himself from one part of the fellowship, had contradicted the heart of gospel (Gal. 2:16-21).

Fellowship was not simply a social gathering for the like-minded.

Has not Peter's offense also been the frequent offense of Christian congregations? It is legitimate to talk of "spiritual equality" while our behavior suggests that others are not full partners in the gospel. The church too often follows Peter's example by not making Christian fellowship concrete. Wherever Christian fellowship is reserved only for people of different tastes and backgrounds, it is hardly Christian fellowship at all. Where the church chooses to separate into segments of black, white, and Mexican-American, it may well repeat Peter's offense.

SINS OF THE FLESH

There is a line in Chaim Potok's *The Promise* where a young rabbinical student says to his inclement professor, "You are destroying people with your religiosity." This professor was sincerely dedicated to his religious tradition, but when someone disagreed he would batter them unmercifully. Someone says later of such people, "They were nice people as long as you agreed with them."

Religion can be exploited to make us resentful and jealous. However, our faith should create a loving people who make fellowship possible. It is often in the name of religion that our fellowship is torn apart.

This was the situation in the Galatian church. Jewish Christians insisted that Gentile believers first become Jews. They were more than willing to destroy the church for the sake of their own standards. These are the people that Paul warns against the "sins of the flesh"—enmity, strife, jealousy, dissension, and party spirit (Gal. 5:19).

The sins of the flesh are not only sexual sins, as is commonly thought; fleshly sins are those which upset the fellowship. The Christian is not to "give an opportunity to the flesh" as it always disturbs the fellowship. (Gal. 5:13).

LIFE IN THE SPIRIT

The Christian lives by a new principle, the principle of the Spirit. Life in the Spirit shows those qualities which build up the fellowship: love, joy, peace, patience, kindness, goodness, faithfulness, gentleness, and self-control (Gal. 5:13-24).

The Galatian church was in immediate danger of being torn apart by some who insisted that Gentiles comply with certain Jewish requirements, such as circumcision. Paul argues in Galatians 5–6 that these ceremonies do not matter. What matters is "faith working through love" (Gal. 5:6).

Christians are called upon to exhibit a unique new

style of life. They are "a new creation" (Gal. 6:15). Strife, jealousy, and party spirit come naturally, for they belong to the carnal life of the flesh. What is called for in the church is the crucifixion of fleshly desire and the resurrection of that love which the Spirit creates (Gal. 5:22). This love generates fellowship and is the only answer to a divided church.

However, love is much easier talked about than put into practice. The constant temptation of the Christian is to resume the unloving life of the flesh. That is why Paul says, "You were called to freedom, brethren; only do not use your freedom as an opportunity for the flesh, but through love be servants of one another" (Gal. 5:13).

Love seeks not its own will. Love leads us, as the Greek literally says, "to become each other's slaves (5:13). Life in the flesh produces an arrogance that disturbs and splits the community. The "self-deceit," "provoking of one another," and "envy" mentioned in Galatians 5:26 have no place in the life of the Spirit.

IMPRISONED BY PRIDE

Doctrinal issues debated in the church can be so heavily tinged with the pride of the opponents that little communication takes place. Such self-conceit creates a spirit which cannot afford to be wrong. Pride is the source of many of the issues which destroy fellowship.

Against this arrogance which separates brothers, Paul says "through love be servants of one another" (Gal 5:13). This advice must have seemed strange to Paul's audience. The lowest level of the social ladder was the slave whose time was spent serving others.

102

Indeed, Aristotle said that a free man is one "who exists for himself and not for another." Paul's position is just the opposite. To be free is to be a slave for others! The whole law is summed up in the words, "Love your neighbor as yourself" (Gal. 5:14).

Authentic love is made concrete in the church when the Spirit enables us to rid ourselves of arrogance. As long as we live by the flesh, we will be ruled by jealousy and conceit. But the new life in Jesus Christ allows us to serve each other (Gal. 5:13-25).

LIKE WILD ANIMALS

To "bite and devour one another" comes quite naturally for the fleshly man. He finds himself divided by the discord which arrogance produces. The church is forever in danger of "devouring one another" as did the Galatians. The language of Galatians 5:15 is graphic. The words "bite" (*dakno*) and "devour" (*katesthio*) are the words for describing the devouring done by wild animals. Where the church lives by this mutual devouring, it will annihilate itself.

The church is faced with a choice: either it is bound together in a grisly, mutual annihilation or it is bound together in mutual, serving love. The only thing which can hold the community together is the love which creates fellowship (Gal. 5:13-15).

The life of the Spirit shows those qualities which build up the fellowship.

How does this love become concretely manifest in

the church? If love means anything at all, it means that brothers should be concerned for the reform of an errant member of the community (Gal. 6:1-10). The community can never be a loving church as long as it is so impersonal and anonymous that errant members are never missed.

The church of the twentieth century provides a special service wherever it exhibits a loving concern that does not reduce people to numbers. Paul would have been highly dissatisfied with that kind of church life which does not make provisions for people to care for each other.

Paul calls upon those who are spiritual to help erring Christians. The real test of having the Spirit is seen in very practical terms. To have the Spirit is to be compassionate. Spiritual people should "set him right" (NEB) with "gentleness," one of the marks of the Spirit's presence. Where the Spirit is present, there can never be apathy toward an erring brother (Gal. 6:1).

BEARING ANOTHER'S BURDEN

Paul's concern with restoring a wayward brother is only one example of the mutual concern which he describes as "bearing one another's burdens" (Gal. 6:2). No one can rightly divorce his own spiritual life from his life in the church. Nor can he congratulate himself on his spiritual superiority over his erring brother. Paul suggests that love never "rejoices in the wrong" (Gal. 6:1-4, KJV; 1 Cor. 13:6). His convictions are illuminated by 1 Corinthians 12:25-26: "The members may have the same care for one another. If one member suffers, all suffer together."

Brotherly love is no empty phrase. Where the

Spirit creates love, a community can be found that bears each other's burdens.

The loneliness in which many of us live makes it more necessary than in the past that we find a caring community. Many of us live in cities where we are likely not to know the names of our neighbors. We are removed from close relatives by distance. We have nothing which can be called our own special community.

A church which lives by the power of the Spirit is the one place where there can remain a sense of intimacy with a caring fellowship. To be sure, too many churches still "bite and devour one another." The Galatians message is that the church is challenged to overcome the natural inclination for discord. Love must create in us mutual concern.

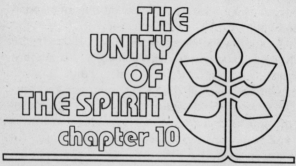

THE UNITY OF THE SPIRIT

chapter 10

"For he is our peace."   Ephesians 2:14

A casual observation of the news on any given day serves as a reminder of how bitterly divided the human family is. Our own nation has lived through several convulsive periods. And the Kerner Commission informed us some years ago that we now have "two societies, one white and one black."

People are also divided along racial and ethnic lines in other parts of the world. In the Middle East two ancient neighbors, the Arab and the Jew, live in mutual distrust and hatred. There is in Northern Ireland a persistent feud between the native Irish Catholics and the Protestant settlers. In Cyprus there has been a long struggle between Greek and Turk. No international organization has been able to create harmony out of chaos.

Around the world, dividing walls of hostility separate group from group. The chief source of hostility seems to be the limits we set on our concern for others. We live with dividing walls all around us.

Where does the church stand in this divided world? The same divisions which exist in the larger society also exist in the church. Like the rest of society, churches tend to be divided by social class, race, and education. There are congregations composed primarily of the upper classes, just as there are churches for the lower classes. There are white churches as well as black churches, status churches as well as nonstatus churches.

Is this prevailing situation to be accepted as normal for the church? Or should the church be uneasy that it is divided along economic, racial, and class lines? One letter in the New Testament addresses this problem—the letter to the Ephesians.

Ephesians was addressed to a world that was rigidly divided between Jew and Greek, slave and free, male and female (Gal. 3:28). It was a world of distinctions between social groups. Against this background, the Ephesian letter is unique in its emphasis on the unity found in Jesus Christ: "He is our peace, having made us both one" (Eph. 2:14; cf. Eph. 2:16; 4:4).

A NEW FELLOWSHIP

In the church a new fellowship exists that is nothing less than a spiritual marvel. This marvel is the focus of Ephesians. It says there is no relationship to Jesus Christ which does not also include fellowship with others.

What kind of fellowship constitutes this oneness? Is it achieved when the church has such periodic social gatherings as a picnic or church party? The church is tempted to see its fellowship in such superficial terms and to go no further in maintaining its unity. But if that is the extent of its unity, the church has succeeded in doing nothing more than is commonly done in a civic club. Many groups foster a sense of belonging on the civic club level, where people of similar backgrounds come together to renew acquaintances and make social contacts.

The fellowship described in Ephesians, however, is far different from that which exists in social organizations. The unique nature of Christian fellowship is indicated in Ephesians 2:11-12, the heart of the letter. Fellowship is to be seen against the natural state of hostility that prevails everywhere in the world.

This passage sounds as if it had been written in our own time. It describes the hostility and alienation which exist between human groups everywhere. Whereas these verses speak of the dividing walls which separated Gentiles from Jews, one needs only to change the names to see just how contemporary they are. Our society, like theirs, is divided. But the fellowship described is adequate to overcome this hostility.

NO ROOM FOR BARRIERS

Fellowship cannot be created by our own ingenuity. The emphasis should be on the One who has brought these hostile groups together. "He is himself our peace. Gentiles and Jews, he has made the two one, and in his own body of flesh and blood he has broken down the enmity which stood like a dividing wall between them" (Eph. 2:14, NEB).

The human mind harbors prejudices that exist like

walls to separate us. We naturally create such walls to separate ourselves from those who are different: blacks from whites, rich from poor, educated from uneducated. In the words of a recent popular song, "Most of us hate anything that we can't understand."

Christ has knocked down our walls of hostility! He has left us vulnerable to others. His cross was the point at which those walls were destroyed. His death for all men affirms that Jesus accepts us all. He has left no room for the barriers which separate us from each other.

Words like peace and reconciliation have long been applied to the story of the cross. We have "peace with God" (Rom. 5:1). "In Christ God was reconciling the world to himself" (2 Cor. 5:19).

We cannot be at peace with God and remain alienated from others.

Before the writing of Ephesians the early church knew that the cross had brought peace and reconciliation between man and God. But Ephesians 2:18 said something new and different. They were told that through Christ the hostile and warring peoples were to have peace and reconciliation with each other.

We all—Jews and Arabs, blacks and whites —come to God together. There is no private route to God; he has no favorites. We cannot be at peace with God and remain alienated from others.

Is there evidence anywhere that the walls have been broken down? Against the backdrop of racial hostility as deep as that which exists in our own time,

Ephesians reveals a wonder of the Spirit (2:14-22). Jews and Gentiles together "have access to God through the one Spirit" and have been reconciled "in one body" (2:16, 18).

There was no room for two separate but equal churches. Such separation would have been a renunciation of the Christ who died to bring them together. In a world that found dividing walls everywhere, the church was evidence that people could be reconciled to each other.

Is the church today a witness to God's reconciling work? Is it a reminder that Christ knocks down the dividing walls which men erect? Or do the same walls which exist outside the church also make their presence known in the Christian community? Ephesians proclaims a Christ who died to knock down the walls of distrust and prejudice. There is no room in the church for these barriers.

THE MIRACLE OF THE CROSS

The church has not always lived to maintain the unity so vigorously announced in Ephesians 2:13-18. We live at times as if the miracle of the cross had not broken through.

In our worship assemblies it often becomes clear that reconciliation has not become a reality. There remain churches that are low income and churches which have social position. But even more disheartening is the fact that people who come to worship with a church whose economic or social base is different from their own situation often feel uncomfortable or even unwelcome. We still live with walls created by sociological, racial, or economic differences.

Ephesians 2:14 calls for us to break down every possible wall that separates men and women from each other. It is never enough to claim that fellowship is a spiritual unity reserved for the next life, while we allow walls to divide us on earth.

To confess Christ is to affirm by our actions the end of separation and alienation. The church exists to demonstrate Christ's reconciling power.

This reconciliation which takes place within the church does not mean that distinctions of sex and race cease to exist, for we remain male and female, black and white. Economic distinctions will remain. But Ephesians reminds us that we can, with our distinctions, live together. Those who are separated by a wall can live together in peace. Wherever there are churches divided by human barriers—we fail to live up to our calling in Jesus Christ.

THE UNITY OF THE SPIRIT

The core of the letter is that Christ has done through the church what no human institution could do. What holds us together is no super organization, administration, planning board, or journal. Our unity results from the fact that there is "one body and one Spirit, just as you were called to the one hope that belongs to your call" (Eph. 4:4). Our unity results from the fact that there is "one Lord, one faith, one baptism," as well as one God (4:5).

The unity of Christians is a divine gift. It rests on something stronger than organizations or creeds. Unity is a gift that is not to be taken lightly.

This gift is precious, and we are told to "Make every effort to keep the unity of the Spirit through the bond of peace" (Eph. 4:3, NIV). The unity

111

granted to us has to be treasured and preserved. We can easily destroy Christ's gift by allowing dividing walls back into the church. The task of the church is to make every effort to maintain the unity Christ has given.

Experience tells us there is more than one kind of unity. There is the unity we see in some societies where authoritarian rulers dictate the terms of unity. In a sense, then, one can speak of the unity of Stalin's Russia or Hitler's Germany. Another type of unity exists where the large majority of people are simply apathetic about the decisions of the few.

We live at times as if the miracle of the cross had not broken through.

The unity envisioned in Ephesians 4, however, cannot be found in either of these types. The unity of the church is maintained by every Christian.

The fact that each Christian has a decisive role to play in maintaining unity becomes clear in Ephesians 4:7-16. Every Christian, or "saint," is devoted "to the work of ministry."

Here we must notice that earlier translations of the New Testament placed the comma at an unfortuante place in verse 12 (after "saints"), leaving the impression that only special persons do the "work of the ministry" and cooperate in the building of the body. Now, almost all translations agree with the emphasis of the RSV (second edition) which reads "to equip the saints for the work of ministry."

Every Christian does play an important role in building up the church. In Ephesians 4:16 the church is a body "jointed and knit together by *every* joint with which it is supplied, when *each* part is working properly. . . ." The unity of the church is neither dictatorial unity nor the unity of apathy. It is created when *each* is devoted to building up the body of Christ.

UNITY THROUGH DIVERSITY

Some have the impression that the unity of the church becomes real when diversity is destroyed. We may even think the ideal church is where all of the members think and act the same. So some churches are threatened by diversity. But the church's diversity is the dynamic which creates unity (Eph. 4:7-16)!

The body cannot function without the interdependent relations of all its parts. Not even one tiny ligament of the body is dispensable, as Paul reminded the Corinthians (1 Cor. 12:18ff.). Just as the diversity of the human body creates its unity, the unity of the church is established by the harmonious relationships of its parts.

Church unity is dependent upon the unique abilities and personalities of each member. The early church needed all kinds—apostles, prophets, evangelists, pastors, and teachers—to be what Christ intended. Today the church needs its young people, old people, executives, workers, blacks, and whites. To "keep the unity" is to use our widely different abilities for the good of the whole body.

We often adopt a scale of values by which we measure and compare the worth of various abilities. Public gifts, such as preaching and teaching, are considered more valuable than others. Thus, we are tempted to consider some members more valuable

113

than others. But the unity described in Ephesians 4 is quite democratic. Each part of the body is indispensable. The church cannot maintain God-given unity and stability until it matures and adopts a new scale of values (Eph. 4:14).

CONSTRUCTIVE LIFE-STYLE

There is a Christian life-style which, when developed by all Christians, adds to the unity of the church. Elements of the pre-Christian life have to be set aside if we "grow into him" and if we are all to attain "the unity of the faith" (Eph. 4:13, 15). There are patterns of behavior learned in Jesus Christ which produce the fellowship of the church.

There are patterns of behavior learned in Jesus Christ which produce the fellowship of the church.

There is the fellowship of *truthfulness,* for instance. Walls of deceit naturally separate people from each other. Where the walls have not been torn down, we are not inclined to open up our lives to others. So we hide behind walls of deceit.

Such walls have no place in the Christian community. Because we are all parts of the same body, we are to put away all "falsehood" and "speak the truth" with each other (Eph. 4:25). Christ has granted us a fellowship and torn down the walls of deceit. As a result we are enabled to live in a community where we are unashamed to be truthful. Only because we live in a supportive and understanding community do we dare to "speak the truth."

114

We must admit, however, that we have not attained a life totally free of deceit. We are still children who have not yet learned to be totally open with each other. Nevertheless we must make the attempt to grow up in such a way as to accomplish the fellowship of truthfulness (Eph. 4:14, 15).

THE FELLOWSHIP OF KINDNESS

Ephesians also speaks of the fellowship of *kindness*. This kind of fellowship has to be taken seriously, for antisocial offenses such as "bitterness and wrath and clamor and slander" belong to the *pre*-Christian life (Eph. 4:31). They build up dividing walls and destroy the unity of the body of Christ. In place of such antisocial habits, the new life calls us to "be kind to one another, tenderhearted, forgiving one another," just as God has forgiven us in Jesus Christ (4:32).

There is also the fellowship of *forgiveness*. It is the habit of the world to bear grudges. Forgiveness does not come naturally. We find it easier to build a wall when someone wrongs us than to tear it down. But at this point the church finds the capacity to do what does not come naturally. Because, we are a forgiven people (Eph. 4:31ff.).

At the cross God forgave us when we deserved no forgiveness. Thus, we who have been forgiven have learned that the new life involves communicating God's acceptance to others. Because he has accepted us, we can accept others. Gratitude for our own forgiveness is demonstrated each time we forgive a brother or sister.

The walls have been broken down and replaced with the unity of the Spirit. Together we all

—teenagers and middle-aged people, blacks and whites, educated and uneducated—have been accepted into *this church without walls*. We now have the task of being certain that we allow no walls to segregate members from each other. We live with a temptation to create these barriers. But to be loyal to Jesus Christ is to be a builder of a church without walls.

A PILGRIM PEOPLE

chapter 11

"Not neglecting to meet together . . . ."

Hebrews 10:25

The letter to the Hebrews was written to a very discouraged people. We know little about either the writer or the recipients of this letter. But we can ascertain enough from the letter itself to know that the readers had become weary of the Christian calling. Although there is never a suggestion that these readers were considering conversion to another faith, such as Judaism, the book is full of suggestions that they were thinking of giving up the faith.

The author of Hebrews writes a "word of exhortation" to encourage his people not to abandon the faith (Heb. 13:22). He is deeply concerned with the subject of fellowship. As the author knows, only when the church is a closely-knit community can it survive in an alien world.

From scattered references in the letter we can see more clearly what church problem prompted the author's response. The readers had "tasted the heavenly gift" but were considering apostasy (Heb. 6:4). They had simply given up all hope in the future promise (4:1; 6:18f.).

The result in Hebrews 10:25 is that many of the Christians had ceased to attend the assembly, for it seemed that the public assembly was irrelevant to their lives. The author's task was to motivate this faltering community to "lift your drooping hands and strengthen your weak knees" (12:12).

It was not an easy task. Those who have tried to motivate dying churches to action know the author was faced with a serious problem. How could he motivate his people to attend public worship? What means were open to encourage them not to give up hope? Was the author's best approach to use new public relations tactics to motivate his people to action? Or was he to appeal to their guilt and frighten them back? The author's response may seem novel to us; he reminded them of the nature of the Christian community.

NO PRIVATE PILGRIMAGE

The readers of the letter may have thought they could maintain their Christian identity apart from the rest of the church. This view was commonly held in some religious circles. Philo, the author's contemporary in Alexandria, spoke of the soul's private pilgrimage to God. Other religious thinkers had divorced religion from life in community.

But the author paints quite a different picture. No private pilgrimages to God are reflected in the Hebrew letter. The church's experience of weariness reminds the author of Israel in the wilderness. Consequently, he describes the Christian life consistently as a pilgrimage, a pilgrimage of the whole church. Individual souls do not go alone to God; instead, the whole church is the pilgrim people of God.

The church stands where Israel once stood, waiting for the promised land. "Good news came to us just as to them" (Heb. 4:2). But the church also stands in danger of repeating the apostasy of Israel (3:6, 12; 4:2).

A PEOPLE ON THE WAY

One needs only to read casually through the letter to see how much the author looks upon the church as a people on the way. The church is compared to the wilderness generation (Heb. 3–4). Jesus is the "pioneer" or "pathfinder" who leads the way (2:10). The great heroes of faith in chapter 11 were always "on the way," looking for a better habitation (11:9, 13–16). The whole church has repeated the pilgrimage of the wilderness generation (12:18). Thus the whole church must "lift (its) drooping hands, strengthen (its) weak knees, and make straight paths" (12:12-13a).

To be a Christian is to belong to the community that is always on its way. There is no pilgrimage without the community; the strength to continue exists only when community members care for each other. To be left alone along the way would be disastrous. The only way to reach the destination is in the care of the community.

The image of the church as a pilgrim people may

seem quaint and even dated to us. We cannot easily envision a nomadic people who are always on the move and who have no firm roots. Yet this image says something about the nature of the church that is frequently lost when we use modern metaphors to describe the church.

There is a unity among the pilgrim people that is not likely to be found among modern institutions and groups. Willie Loman, in Arthur Miller's *The Death of a Salesman* observes that people can become either too old or too ill to maintain their function, and thus they are discarded. "You can't take the orange and throw away the peel," he cries. When the author of Hebrews describes the church as the pilgrim people, he has in mind a people who struggle together and travel together. Even under uncertain conditions they care for each other when illness and sickness threaten.

Only when the church is a closely-knit community can it survive in an alien world.

This description of the church as the pilgrim people is especially meaningful in our time, for our society has become increasingly nomadic. Few societies are as mobile as the present American society. The result of this mobility is a disturbing loss of long-time relationships. The fact that we move frequently may even prevent us from establishing close relationships when we move to a new place.

This loss of close friendships means that in times of sickness or grief, relatives and friends are no longer there to help. Perhaps it is just here that the church, itself composed of highly mobile people, can provide the warmth and assistance that are needed. The Christian community of today, like the recipients of Hebrews, is on the move. Here there is a ministry for those who are injured along the way.

What are the pilgrim people to do? How does the church respond when its members become apathetic and weary? The Hebrew letter is a treatise on holding the church together. It is a lesson for the contemporary church to hear.

WHEN PEOPLE DROP OUT

If the church is the pilgrim people, it is inevitable that among these pilgrims there will be those who impede the progress of the entire group. Some will decide that the effort is too much, and will drop out. Others will see that the "race" has turned out to be a distance run and not a sprint, and they will want to quit (Heb. 12:1-2). Others will become injured, lame or ill along the way (12:13). Every church is faced with this problem. What can the pilgrim people do when people drop out?

First, there is a word of caution. "Take care, brethren, lest there be in any of you an evil, unbelieving heart," says the author (Heb. 3:12). "While the promise of entering his rest remains, let us fear lest any of you be judged to have failed to reach it" (4:1). "See to it that no one fail to obtain the grace of God; that no 'root of bitterness' spring up and cause trouble, . . . that no one be immoral or irreligious like Esau . . ." (12:15-16).

Scattered throughout the letter is a singular emphasis. The Greek word *tis*, which means "any," appears in each of these passages. It emphasizes the

121

importance of the individual on the pilgrimage. The author's concern is not only with the church as an institution; but also with each individual. It is not enough for the church to reach its destination; there is the concern "lest any" drop out.

The church fails its task when it becomes impersonal and loses touch with individual members. The institutions of our society may reduce people to numbers in the computer. Corporations and academic institutions may become indifferent to individuals. But the church, the pilgrim people, should be concerned that "no one fail to obtain the grace of God" (Heb. 12:15). When the church reduces its people to numbers, it has failed its task.

HINDERED BY THE LAME

What happens when the pilgrim people are hindered in their progress by one who is lame? This was inevitable whenever a large community set out on their pilgrimage. There would be present both the young and old, the healthy and the sick. At some point the community would have to decide what to do with the infirm.

Does it leave them along the way? Or does it stop to give aid? The author says, "And make straight paths for your feet, so that what is lame may not be put out of joint but rather be healed" (Heb. 12:13).

The church is a healing community. There are some within the community who are likely to fall away if the church does not provide "straight paths." It is by making "straight paths" that the church can be a healing community. The church's task is to provide the opportunity for its people to find spiritual wholeness when lameness threatens their progress.

How does the community go about its task of healing? The author uses a very expressive verb in Hebrews 12:15 when he says, "See to it that no one fail to obtain the grace of God." The verb translated "see to it" is *episkopeo,* which, in the noun form, is our word for bishop (*episkopos*). This is the term for the overseer who has responsibility for his people.

But when the author summons the church to "see to it" that no one fall away, he is not speaking of the duty of a church leader. He is speaking of the task of the whole church. Every member has the duty to "see to it" that his brother does not fall away from God. The responsibility for others, the task of caring, is not reserved for church officials. The whole church is to fulfil this task.

EXHORT ONE ANOTHER

Closely connected to the author's advice for the community's care for its members is the summons to the church in Hebrews 3:13, "But exhort one another every day." If we recall that the book of Hebrews is itself a "word of exhortation," we will recognize that the chief concern of this letter is the encouragement of a dispirited people. This encouragement is not assigned to a professional minister. It is the mutual ministry of the whole church. This exhortation is not limited to special occasions, for the author calls on the members to encourage each other "every day." Undoubtedly he knows that the physical presence of other Christians is a source of strength that can produce endurance and faith.

Has the contemporary church lost these elements of our life together that were essential to the author's "word of exhortation?" The author knew that the answer to a discouraged people was a caring concern by members for each other. If the members failed to demonstrate this care, there was no power which could hold the community together.

The fellowship of caring extends beyond simple concern for the discouraged. There are also those who have had to suffer in a difficult situation.

The church's task is to provide the opportunity for its people to find spiritual wholeness when lameness threatens their progress.

In the author's day some Christians were imprisoned because of their faith (Heb. 10:34). Such a situation might cause some to keep their distance from an imprisoned brother. A Christian might have thought it best for the church to remain respectable, thus isolating their less fortunate brother. But the author says, "Remember those who are in prison, as though in prison with them; and those who are ill-treated, since you also are in the body" (13:3). The church does not keep its distance from Christian prisoners!

Moreover, to remember such people meant far more than to think about their condition. The author has in mind active involvement. Indeed, we identify with the fate of those who are less fortunate "as though in prison with them." The author would have agreed with Paul's statement that "if one member suffers, all suffer together" (1 Cor. 12:26). The Christian fellowship shares not only in joy, but also in misfortune.

We can imagine that the earliest Christians, often excluded from the civic and social life of the ancient world, found considerable strength in their common life together. Indeed, some pagan writers looked on in amazement at the communal ties which bound Christians together, even in misfortune. This depth of fellowship also served an evangelistic purpose, for ancient peoples were impressed with the demonstration of such love for each other.

This kind of fellowship which shared even in misfortune can also be the power of Christianity in our depersonalized world. Undoubtedly many people are attracted to the faith more by the experience of being loved than by persuasive arguments. The author found in this deep fellowship of misfortune a power by which to encourage a defeated people.

THE FELLOWSHIP OF WORSHIP

What does attendance at worship have to do with the Christian life? Can one live the Christian life without being a part of a worshiping community? Only the letter to the Hebrews deals with this question.

Among the readers of this letter there was the growing temptation to neglect the assembly. Hebrews 10:25 suggests some had already done so. We cannot be sure what had caused them to neglect the public worship. Perhaps it was the result of a general apathy. Or perhaps a feeling of superiority to the rest of the community led these Christians from the public worship. Or there could have been the feeling that "nothing happened" at the public assembly. Whatever the cause of this neglect of public worship, the author considers the matter serious enough to direct his readers' attention to the subject.

First, he gives the charge to his readers, "and let us consider how to stir up one another to love and good works, not neglecting to meet together . . ." (Heb. 10:24-25). Love and good works are not produced in a vacuum. Individuals do not frequently inspire themselves to action. But there is an infectious ability in the group to incite us to action. It is for this reason that public worship is important.

Many people are attracted to the faith more by the experience of being loved than by persuasive arguments.

There should be a power in the public proclamation, in singing, and even in the contact with others that can instill an enthusiasm unavailable apart from public worship. Thus, in the context of comments about the public worship, the author says the brethren should be "encouraging one another." Public worship is important because each Christian needs to be "stirred up" to love and good works. To miss the assembly is to miss an opportunity for the nurturing of the whole church.

The author's comments suggest that something happens in public worship which does not depend on the impressiveness of the sermon or the singing (though good preaching and singing never hurt!). We might also conclude that attendance does not grow out of a strict sense of duty. Worship is important because "one loving heart sets another on fire."

It is this attitude toward worship which apathetic contemporary churches could use. There are reasons for regular attendance at worship that are far better than those which have traditionally been given. To worship is to renew our relationship to the whole community.

SHARE WHAT YOU HAVE

There was one particular act in worship which underlined the unity of the church. We have observed already that the early church practiced a fellowship of means in which resources were shared (Acts 2:44-45). This act was called "fellowship" (*koinonia*) because of the mutual sharing with people became apparent.

Apparently the author of Hebrews saw in this practice a way of making fellowship real. He says, "Do not neglect to do good and to share what you have, for such sacrifices are pleasing to God" (Heb. 13:16). Both the expressions "do good" and "share what you have" (*koinonia*) were terms for helping the poor. The church knew that there could be no real fellowship as long as there was a serious economic gap between the rich and the poor. Thus real fellowship was made concrete at regular periods when the rich helped the poor.

There may be occasions today for the contemporary church to practice real fellowship in this concrete way. Fellowship can be hindered where brethren are driven apart by economic differences But fellowship can be strengthened where brethren "share what they have."

ENRICHING LIFE TOGETHER
chapter 12

"Confess your faults to one another."

James 5:16

No book of the New Testament is as practical in content as James. It is a collection of practical admonitions for our life together in the church. James is addressed, not to a specific church, but to churches everywhere—the twelve tribes in the Dispersion. Precisely because this book contains practical advice, we may expect it to say something about fellowship that will help us improve the quality of our life together.

There is a constant temptation in the Christian fellowship to seek favor with those who are especially influential. We sometimes forget that Christ has created a fellowship without normal social distinctions.

Apparently the readers of this letter were faced

with such a temptation. James maintains a consistent warning against the rich who abuse others (James 5:1-6) and against the covetous spirit which is more concerned with buying and trading than with God (4:13-17). Such an admiration for wealth can easily damage the Christian fellowship, leading to favoritism toward those who are wealthy.

HAVING STATUS WITH GOD

The author imagines, in James 2, a situation that may sound like an incident in any conteporary congregation. Suppose, he says, a rich man and a poor man come simultaneously into your assembly. The rich man is pictured in this instance as wearing gold rings, which indicates that he is of senatorial rank or is a Roman nobleman. Only such men had the right to wear the gold ring. He is also portrayed as wearing fine clothing—a white toga. Such robes were worn by candidates for elective office.

The readers would recognize the rich man as a member of the aristocracy. They might easily consider that it would be beneficial to the church to have the proper connections. The rich man in question might even be useful in improving the church's status in town. The church in turn might give support to this candidate and create a cozy relationship!

The situation mentioned by James sounds modern indeed. The church is always faced with similar temptations. It may be able to rationalize its position and consider how much more useful, in the long run, would be the support of a wealthy prospect.

We may be tempted to spend more energies converting the influential person than we would in converting the poor person. We may even play an interesting game with numbers and say, "If only we could convert such influential people, imagine how much faster we could convert the others in our midst!" James has, without doubt, seen one of the serious temptations which faces the church.

Favoritism ... has no place in the Christian community.

Sociologists have observed the tendency for congregations and even whole denominations to divide along economic and class lines. There are churches of the rich and churches of the poor. Seldom, however, do we see congregations where economic and class distinctions are forgotten.

The church has too frequently succumbed to the temptation mentioned by James—to say to the rich man, "Have a seat here, please," while it says to the poor, "Stand there" (James 2:3). James asks, "Have you not made distinctions among yourselves? . . ." (2:4). The same question confronts us in our congregations today.

BE WARMED AND FILLED
Favoritism is a natural feature of ordinary communities, but, according to James, it has no place in the Christian community. the reason is that normal Christian behavior has been established by God. God is not partial: "Has not God chosen those who are poor in the world to be rich in faith and heirs of the kingdom which he has promised to those who love him?" (James 2:5).

The Christian community is different from all human communities because it finds its standard in

130

the activity of God. The God of biblical faith has a special attachment to the downtrodden (1 Cor. 1:26-28). The community that he has called into existence is summoned to reflect the behavior of the impartial God.

James also gives a second reason for the community to be impartial. Partiality is a violation of that command which is the heart of God's law, "You shall love your neighbor as yourself" (Lev. 19:18; Matt. 22:39; Rom. 13:9).

It is not enough to claim that we love our neighbor: we must make this love concrete. Jesus explains the meaning of this command by telling the story of the good Samaritan. James explains that this command is to be put into practice when the church erases the distinctions between rich and poor. To love our neighbor is to see him, even when he is poverty-stricken, as a creature of dignity, as one for whom Christ died.

The church does not produce community by heaping up pious phrases about peace and brotherhood.

This relationship of rich and poor, which is important elsewhere in the New Testament, lies at the heart of James' admonitions concerning faith and works (Gal 2:10; Acts 11:29-30). Apparently the "faith only" people of this letter were the ones who would greet their hungry brother with the empty words, "Go in peace" and "be warmed and filled" (James 2:16).

The church, as James suggests, does not produce

131

community by heaping up pious phrases about peace and brotherhood. Real community becomes a reality where there is a concrete concern for "the needs of the body"within the whole church.

THE TONGUE IN THE BODY

If there is ever to be a sense of community in the church, teachers and public leaders must assume an awesome responsibility. The fellowship of the church does not simply happen. Where a healthy relationship among members exists it is usually because responsible church leaders have worked to maintain this unity. Conversely, where a church cannot maintain the fellowship in peace, some responsibility (though not the only responsibility) must lie with church leaders.

James gives a strong warning about the use of the tongue (3:3-12) immediately after he says, "Let not many of you become teachers. . .for you know that we who teach shall be judged with greater strictness" (3:1). There are serious risks in accepting the responsibility of a church leader.

James, who knows well the problems of community, realizes that nothing can be as destructive to genuine community as an irresponsible leader or teacher. Such a person can use his powers of persuasion to exploit differences in the congregation to his own personal advantage. His pulpit or lectern can be the forum for announcing his own frustrations, hatreds, and prejudices.

James compares the leader's tongue to the tiny spark which can set a whole forest on fire (3:5-6). We have seen, in the works of a demagogue like Hitler, the explosive power of the tongue. The tongue also can be explosive in the congregation. Everyone, members and leaders alike, should recognize that he has the power either to disrupt or to build the church.

THE LEADER'S TEMPTATION

A further aspect of the leader's temptation is that he may be tempted to confuse his place with God's place. He may be certain that he is God's spokesman, certain of his own infalliblity. Every disagreement with a brother becomes a righteous cause, and everyone who disagrees is considered a heretic. The leader must recognize his own fallibility and use his ability to build and not to destroy.

The church needs responsible leaders who will mature sufficiently to guide the whole church through their public ministry. James even says that the person who can control his tongue can "bridle the whole body" (3:2), the church.

The leader can be the tongue of the church. He is a very small member, but like the bit in the horse's mouth and like the tiny rudder on a big ship, the leader can give the direction which holds the community together (3:3-4). By setting the tone of the church, he helps to determine whether the church lives in peace or whether it is forever divided.

Not only must leaders learn the fellowship of tongue control, but the whole community must refrain from destructive speech:

Do not speak evil against one another, brethren. He that speaks evil against a brother or judges his brother, speaks evil against the law . . . who are you that you judge your neighbor?
James 4:11-12.

A unique idea is presented here: to speak against a brother is to speak against God's law. Because God's word is directed to all people without distinctions, whether rich or poor, educated or uneducated, rejection of a brother is a rejection of the gospel itself. God has called us all into fellowship, and the Christian is not to destroy the fellowship through careless speech.

There is little doubt that careless gossip, some of which is merely thoughtless, is a major source of breakdown in Christian fellowship. Jealousies can be exploited by the planting and relaying of a damaging story.

Our destructive speech may even appear in the guise of help or good will. On occasion we may condemn another by faint praise ("He does a good job, considering his ability"). In all these instances, the letter of James reminds us that the cause of unity is best served by the prudent tongue.

FELLOWSHIP IN PRAYER

Perhaps the quality of the Christian fellowship is never known until misfortune comes. Misfortune tests whether the church's life together is superficial or real.

When sickness or tragedy occurs, Christian fellowship is tested. In too many circumstances today sickness has become the concern of the physician, not of the church. Where a community of Christians becomes so depersonalized in their way, the church finds it difficult to become actively involved with the pain and suffering of its members.

As long as the church is incapable of caring for the sufferer, it has not broken through to establish real fellowship. James speaks of a fellowship where the elders of the church went to those Christians who were ill to anoint them with oil, in the traditional custom of that day (James 5:14; cf. Mark 6:13; Luke 10:34).

The elders used the means at their disposal to care for one of their own. Those who were in either physical or mental pain were not ignored; they were never allowed to suffer alone. They belonged to a caring fellowship.

The extent of this caring is further suggested by James' confidence in intercessory prayer. Not only was the sick person anointed; the elders also were told to pray for such a person. The whole church was encouraged to "pray for one another" (5:16).

The cause of unity is best served by the prudent tongue.

There is power in intercession. One can imagine that in the church James envisions, there was regular prayer in which disciples were mentioned by name. The intercession was neither general nor impersonal. In this act of interceding for one another, the church was empowered to achieve real fellowship.

Contemporary congregations must learn that community lives and dies by the prayers of members for each other. When we make a regular practice of interceding, we can no longer condemn that brother for whom we pray. Nor can we be apathetic toward the burden of that person.

To intercede is to bring our brother into the presence of God, to see him as a poor sinner in need of grace. It is to ask that our brother receive the same

135

mercy from God that we have received. Such intercession actually creates fellowship.

CONFESS TO ONE ANOTHER

The community will find, if it looks very far, that there are some who suffer from disturbances that are not merely physical. Christians find themselves burdened with guilt, alone with their sins, and afraid to bring them before the group for fear of being rejected. They picture the church as a gathering only for the pious, little knowing that the church is composed of redeemed sinners.

How do we avoid the tragedy and hypocrisy of living alone with our sin? James answers, "Confess your sins to one another" (James 5:16).

There can never be a genuine Christian fellowship until we can accept ourselves and each other as sinners. Where this is the case we no longer have to hide ourselves up in the presence of others, knowing that this is the one community which will accept us despite our failures.

Has the church accepted its mission to become an accepting place where people can admit their guilt? In the work of Jesus, in his table fellowship with sinners, the church should catch the vision of what it is called to be.

The Lord who accepted sinners summons the church to be the place where sinners can admit that they are sinners. Just as Alcoholics Anonymous accepts into its number those who admit their problem, the church is a company of sinners who accept others who confess their sins.

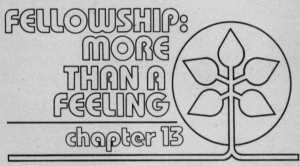

FELLOWSHIP: MORE THAN A FEELING
chapter 13

"*Do not let what you eat cause the ruin of one for whom Christ died.*"

Romans 14:15

This study of the corporate life of the church has a twofold purpose. First, it is intended to help us grasp what biblical fellowship really is. We can hope that when we speak of the fellowship of the church, our understanding will be derived from a truly biblical point of view, and not from popular misconceptions.

Second, we can hope that our encounter with the biblical view of fellowship will give us a sense of urgency to examine our church life and recover a genuine partnership in the gospel. We have seen that the fellowship which we find in Scripture is by no means an auxiliary function of the church. Fellowship is a major goal of the Christian life. There is, therefore, a necessity that we become the kind of fellowship which the Bible describes.

If we are to recover the biblical dimension of fellowship, there are some important lessons which are needed in the life of the church today. Some of these lessons may serve to correct past misunderstandings about fellowship. Other lessons may seem new and untried to us, while still others may be, at least imperfectly, already a part of our understanding and practice. We can hope that, while our practice of the biblical ideal is imperfect, we are a church on the way toward being a genuine fellowship. The following observations can be derived from our study.

PARTNERS IN A TASK

Although it is a fact that our fellowship together can be enhanced by those occasions where church members meet socially, such occasions are not the full extent of Christian fellowship. Christian fellowship, as we have seen, consists in a partnership in a common task. We are partners or fellows (*koinonoi*) in the work to which we have been called.

Just as Paul found in Titus a partner (2 Cor. 3:8), we are partners in the proclamation of the gospel. Thus if we are to recover the biblical meaning of fellowship, this common life will be realized whenever all of us are active participants in the partnership of the gospel.

We can hope that we will see the urgency of recognizing the church as a community of diverse gifts where each person has a part in its mission. Fellowship will not be genuine and biblical unless there is a role to play by all members. No part of the church —neither young nor old—should exist simply to be entertained.

Respect for individuals as full partners will compel us to be certain that the contribution of each person is expected and appreciated. Nor will the work of the church be simply delegated to a professional staff. Fellowship will be a reality when we are all "parts" in a partnership.

FELLOWSHIP IN PRACTICE

Many of us used to hear about a spiritual fellowship quite unrelated to our daily lives. There were churches which spoke of a spiritual fellowship with other races and nationalities, but were unwilling to make this fellowship a reality in practice. From our study we have learned that the fellowship which Jesus Christ has made possible must be made actual in our lives.

Fellowship will not be genuine and biblical unless there is a role to play by all members.

Peter learned that it did no good to speak of fellowship with Gentiles unless he was willing to sit down to eat with them. In the same way Paul wanted to cement the fellowship between Gentile and Jewish Christians by taking a collection from the wealthier Gentile churches to the poorer Judean churches. In both instances there was the concern that the fellowship which Christ had made possible would be made visible through their activities.

Perhaps we have made some progress in learning that the truth of fellowship has to be put into practice. We can hope that, instead of congratulating ourselves on our progress in recent years, we will continue to demonstrate the truth of the gospel in our daily lives. We may find, as Peter did, that this task is not easy. But Scripture summons us to accept into actual fellowship all whom God has accepted.

AN INCLUSIVE FELLOWSHIP

We sometimes hear Christians speak of the fellowship they have when they meet in a group with others who share the same interests, income level, and educational background. They may be a segment of a congregation or of several congregations. Such a gathering, with people of similar backgrounds, is quite exclusive. Indeed, such people would probably enjoy each other's company without the benefit of their common faith, for they have much in common anyway.

We have seen in this study that Christian fellowship is not exclusive. If our fellowship consists only in a relationship with people who are very much like us, we have reason to ask how the church is different from any other community.

The New Testament regularly shows that the community life of God's people is different, for it is *inclusive*. We need only to recall how Jesus called into fellowship the outcasts of his time to recognize how inclusive is his fellowship. In the same way, we find the early church continually struggling to reflect the inclusiveness of God's call.

We naturally find it easier to exclude those who are different than to include them, as did the Judaizers in the letter to the Galatians. But if fellowship is real, we will go beyond what comes naturally. We will be a fellowship which welcomes people of different age, race, and income groups.

RECEIVE ONE ANOTHER

Fellowship is sometimes spoken of in such a way as to suggest that it extends only to those who agree with us on every conceivable issue. This view has often caused sincere people to be divided behind innumerable barriers.

We have observed in this study that real fellowship extends to people whose opinions differ from our own. The controversy between the *strong* and the *weak* in Romans 14-15 concerns a serious difference of opinion. Nevertheless, both sides are counseled not to "judge one another" (Rom. 14:3). Despite those differences, they are to "receive one another" (Rom. 15:7), knowing that God is the ultimate judge.

There is a particular urgency that we learn to accept those who differ from us, for there can never be a fellowship if we all try to assume God's role as judge. A church which continues to be fragmented into exclusive groups has failed the Lord who died to bring us together.

Yet, while there is room in the church for differences of opinion, the church is not a club where convictions do not matter. We were called into fellowship by the preaching about Jesus. And the conviction that Jesus Christ is Lord has brought the church together.

Paul was very concerned at any point where others threatened to diminish the all-sufficiency of Christ by insisting on obedience to works of the law. Indeed, he accused the Galatian opponents of "preaching another gospel" (Gal. 1:6), and said that Cephas, by his behavior, had betrayed "the truth of the gospel" (Gal. 2:14). Thus, the Christian fellowship is not indifferent to matters of conviction.

The exhortation that we accept those who disagree with us does not mean that there are no limits to fellowship. There are definite limits to fellowship. Passages such as 1 Corinthians 5:1-13, 2 Corinthians 6:14–7:1, 2 John 7–10, Titus 3:8-11, Matthew 18:15-17, and 1 Timothy 1:18-20 address this subject, providing some guidelines for the church. Limits to fellowship cannot be overlooked. But, while there are limits, our fellowship cannot be genuine if we are forever excluding those whose opinions differ from ours.

THE SHEPHERD VALUES HIS SHEEP

Many communities function without any great loss when members come and go. The survival of the group is often more important than the individual. But when we recall the story of the shepherd who left the ninety-nine sheep in order to find the one, we know that we can never lose sight of the individual. We are in fact our brothers' keepers, bearing the burdens of those who fail (Gal. 6:2). Their importance to us is not derived from their ability, or talent, or prestige; it is derived from the fact that they, as individuals, are people for whom Christ died. If we are to recover the biblical practice of fellowship, we will not be caught in a numbers game which ignores the individual.

MORE THAN A FEELING

The close ties of Christians should produce warm and caring relationships between the people of God. But feelings of warmth and affection can be found in many groups. Thus we must not confuse the biblical idea of fellowship with the natural affection for those who are close to us.

We may be practicing biblical fellowship long before we have established a strong sense of warmth for all who are involved in the community. Fellowship is primarily captured by ministering selflessly to fellow members of the body of Christ and sharing a partnership in a common task.

If our fellowship consists only in a relationship with people who are very much like us, we have reason to ask how the church is different from any other community.

Throughout this study we have seen that Christian fellowship possesses a quality that distinguishes it from other groups. If the quality of our life together is not different from that of the civic club, we have not found real Christian fellowship.

Now it is worthwhile for us to ask what makes the difference in the quality of our life together. The answer is that the nature of our life together was determined by God's act in Jesus Christ. So, wherever the early church struggled over the problem of becoming a fellowship, Paul's solution rested on the cross of Christ.

Why should we repress our selfishness in the community? And why not please ourselves to the detriment of the whole community? Paul says that it is because Christ did not please himself at the cross (Rom. 15:3).

Why should we concern ourselves with our weaker brother in the community? It is because each weaker brother is "one for whom Christ died" (Rom. 14:15). That is, the foundation for our fellowship is the cross of Christ. It was there that we learned the real meaning of love and selflessness. This love that was demonstrated at the cross is the foundation of our fellowship. When we live by the cross, our fellowship is unlike any other community.

When we experience this particular quality of life together we can believe that the church which recovers the biblical view of fellowship is an answer to the loneliness of our time. When we learn the message of the cross we will not reduce people to numbers on a computer card. We will not stereotype others by the color of their skin or their income level, for we have learned of the One who accepts us all. Where we are faithful to the gospel, we will be tearing down the dividing walls that separate people from each other.

Christ was our model by striking down the dividing wall of hostility (Eph. 2:14). The Christ who died to create life together summons us to go on with the unfinished task of being the kind of community he intended.